THREEWAYS

Fulfill Your Ultimate Fantasy

THREEWAYS
Fulfill Your
Ultimate
Fantasy

DIANA CAGE

a
alyson books
NEW YORK

MANUFACTURED IN THE UNITED STATES OF AMERICA.

THIS TRADE PAPERBACK ORIGINAL IS PUBLISHED BY ALYSON BOOKS,
P.O. BOX 1253, OLD CHELSEA STATION, NEW YORK, NEW YORK 10113-1251.

DISTRIBUTION IN THE UNITED KINGDOM BY TURNAROUND PUBLISHER SERVICES LTD.,
UNIT 3, OLYMPIA TRADING ESTATE, COBURG ROAD, WOOD GREEN,
LONDON N22 6TZ ENGLAND.

FIRST EDITION: JULY 2006

06 07 08 09 a 10 9 8 7 6 5 4 3 2 1

ISBN 10 15583-939-8
ISBN 13 978-1-55583-939-0

"THROW YOUR OWN SEX PARTY," "MALE SEXUAL ANATOMY," "THE WELL-STOCKED TOY BOX," AND "THE HAPPY ENDING: EROTIC MASSAGE FOR LOVERS" HAVE BEEN REPRINTED OR ADAPTED BY PERMISSION OF WWW.GOODVIBES.COM

AN APPLICATION FOR LIBRARY OF CONGRESS CATALOGING-IN-PUBLICATION DATA HAS BEEN FILED.

ILLUSTRATIONS OF MALE AND FEMALE ANATOMY ARE BY COLLEEN COOVER
COVER PHOTOGRAPH © CORBIS.

BOOK DESIGN BY VICTOR MINGOVITS.

CONTENTS

INTRODUCTION

WE ALL DREAM OF having exciting, adventurous sex with or without a long term partner—sometimes without ever really believing it's possible. I believe that sex is one of the most important aspects of our lives. It's one of the keys to happy long-term relationships, and it's part of feeling happy with our bodies and ourselves. Sex is a way to communicate and learn. Not to mention the fact that it's pleasurable, and we really don't put enough importance on pleasure.

I wrote a book on threeways not so much because I was having tons of them, but because my lovers and partners kept talking about them. Threeways seemed to be a fantasy trope that appeared regularly in my sex life. For a while it seemed like every person I went to bed with was fantasizing about having another person present. And when I started asking around among friends, most concurred that it was their number-one fantasy. There were all variations on the theme. Some people wanted to watch their partner get it on with someone else. Some wanted to have attention lavished on them by two people at once, some wanted a threeway as a way to explore stuff they didn't get to do in their everyday sex lives, some folks wanted to dominate or submit to two people at once. There were so many threeway fantasies among my partners and friends I couldn't figure out why we weren't all having more of them.

One night I had this incredible sex with someone I was dating. I mean, the sex was mind-blowing. We were on the floor of my studio apartment and she was describing a fantasy about a rather elaborate threeway she wanted to have (I think it involved cops, or firefighters, or possibly truckers). All I know is the sex was so hot I couldn't think straight. I got so excited I blurted out *I love you* at one point, though we'd only been together a few months and the "I love you" precedent had yet to be set. I felt like I was in a *Sex and the City* episode where they were trying to decide if it counts to say "I love you" when you are mid-orgasm. We both just sort of looked at the words hanging out there in the air not really knowing what to do about them. So to cover up my effusiveness I decided to try and figure out a way to make my girlfriend's threeway fantasy happen.

And that was when it hit me. The reason everyone was getting off on the idea of threeways but not actually having them is that it was really difficult to orchestrate one. Every time I brought up the name of someone I'd be willing to get down with, she turned up her nose. And everyone she suggested, I hated. We talked about doing it with a stranger, with a pro, with the cable guy, with my ex-girlfriend, with her ex-girlfriend—and all sorts of other possible participants. And we just couldn't agree. We had too much at stake, we didn't feel secure enough, and we were both too scared to take a risk.

I was married to a very open-minded guy throughout my early twenties. He was free of hang-ups about most things and his attitude combined with my own desire for sexual adventure taught me that it was possible to have great sex in a long-term relationship, and to have threeways where no one gets hurt. But our threeways had always been spontaneous. Most of our friends were as relaxed about sex as we were, and we were always falling into and out of multiple-partner situations. It wasn't until I was single and dating that I realized that my sexual utopia was the exception rather than the rule. And though I'd had my share of adventures, I'd never actually planned out anything in advance with a lover. When I looked around for information on the topic of threeways, I found practically none. What little existed was totally homophobic. Usually the information assumed that all threeways followed the two girls and a guy model—not that there's anything wrong with that arrangement, but it didn't fit my all-girl fantasy. It was like it never occurred to anyone that the rest of the world wanted a little ménage à trois action, or that all straight guys who wanted to get into a threeway weren't simply rejects from the *Girls Gone Wild* camera crew.

So, suffice it to say I figured out a few things during my quest for the girlfriend-plus-one sexual arrangement. I learned how to talk to my partner about what I was comfortable with and I learned how to set boundaries so that all three of us ended up happy and sexually sated rather than resentful and disappointed. I learned so much about making it work that I figured I might as well write a book.

You Can Learn a Lot About Sex from Working at a Porn Magazine

During the nearly five years I spent editing the lesbian sex magazine *On Our Backs*, I attended countless photo shoots, watched dozens of couples have sex, reviewed more porn videos then I could possibly count, and wrote articles about everything from rimming to rope bondage. I attended tons of workshops and demos, I read every sex book that came through the office and tried out every sex toy that came across my desk. And every day a reader, another editor, or a freelancer would come to me with a question about sex. And since I was the gal in charge it was my job to figure out the answer.

I was lucky to have the sexy brainiac Tristan Taormino as my editor when I first started at *On Our Backs*. She had this impressive way of talking about sex without any judgment whatsoever. It didn't matter what the topic was, or how outré I found it to be, Tristan could speak on it with sophistication and enthusiasm. I learned a lot from her example, and over the years, as I did more public speaking about sex, and writing on the topic, I realized all my own biases and judgments had started falling away on their own. And suddenly I felt more qualified to talk about sex than I'd ever been before.

Rigid sexual categories, hang-ups, and biases sure take up a lot of space in our bedrooms. And all they really do is keep us from having fun. And when I set out to write a book about threeways, I realized talking about having sex with more than one person would be a perfect way to convince people to start stepping outside their little sexual boxes. A threeway is way more than just fodder for the Spice Channel, it's also an opportunity to learn about yourself and challenge some of your sexual biases.

I firmly believe that we can all get what we want out of sex without getting hurt. And the biggest obstacle most people have to a truly great sex life is an inability to talk about sex combined with a bunch of beliefs left over from seventh grade. Once you start to air that stuff, you realize it's ridiculous. The trick is figuring out how to air it. I don't think I can really instruct anyone on how to let go of a lifetime of unchallenged notions, but I can certainly tell you that everything is a lot more fun once you do.

A Word About the Personal Stories in This Book

I interviewed dozens of couples, triads, and single folks for this book. I posted ads online asking people to tell me their threeway tales and quizzed friends at parties. I talked to sexperts and poly people. I pried into everyone's sex lives for months trying to come up with a set of stories to share with curious readers as well as learn a thing or two myself. And it worked! I learned a lot from the people I spoke to.

Everyone had a story to share. Some people were threeway enthusiasts who wanted to spread the word along with me. Some folks were less experienced but had always wanted to try it out. And lots of people were just eager to share their experience and fantasies. I've included as many of the stories I collected as I could and I think as much can be learned from them as the instructional sections of the book.

•••

This book is written for everyone who wants to have a threeway, regardless of gender, sexual orientation, or relationship status. I want it to be accessible to everyone interested in having a threeway, no matter who or what you want to have it with. I've found myself in threeways of every conceivable gender combo and they've all been a blast. If this book encourages you to step outside of some box you've found yourself in, I'd be more than a little pleased. I hope you enjoy reading it and it helps you go out and make all your threeway fantasies come true.

CHAPTER 1

THREE IS A MAGIC NUMBER

EVERY TIME I THINK about threeways, I think about the *Schoolhouse Rock* song "Three Is a Magic Number." I'm not sure that was the goal of the *Schoolhouse Rock* people, but nevertheless it's stuck in my head. In the song, a series of important combinations of three are pointed out and described as perfectly balanced mystical trinities in some way or another. And it holds true for three people in a bed, too. Four people just split up into couples, five is too much work, and six is an orgy. But three? Three is perfect.

WHY HAVE A THREEWAY?

The obvious answer to why have a threeway is "Why not?" It's one of the most common fantasies out there. There are so many reasons to have a threeway and practically no reasons not to. But the best reason to get it on with two other people has got to be that sex is fun and pleasure is good for you.

A threeway is a great way to add variety to your sex life. Change things up a bit by inviting a new person over to play. Threeways are exciting. Sometimes we're attracted to more than one person at a time. Well, as long as you do it right there's no reason why you shouldn't be able to crawl into bed with them. You'll find that three people can do things that two people can't. When there are more people, there are more arms and legs, hands and mouths, and everything else. It's a great way to indulge either your exhibitionist or voyeuristic tendencies. It's a great way to explore your fantasies, change your routine, and add new tricks to your sex life. We all deserve to have as much sex as we want as often as we want.

And what about the purely hedonistic benefits of a threeway? Sex with two other partners means twice as much attention and twice as much contact. Imagine having a four-hand erotic massage, or two-mouth oral sex. A threeway is about the best way I can think of to get one or more of your erogenous zones stimulated at the same time. If you've even fantasized about being penetrated from both ends, or having your bed piled high with arms and legs, then a threeway is for you. Maybe you've wanted to experiment with BDSM or switch up your normal role by topping if you are usually on the bottom, or vice versa. A threeway is the perfect scenario in which to make this kind of thing happen. One of my past lovers got off on the idea of spanking another girl while I watched. In fact, so many of my lovers' masturbatory fantasies have involved more than one girl it's a wonder we ever had one-on-one sex. A threeway simply affords you options that partner sex doesn't.

> *I have threeways because I've yet to meet one man with two dicks far enough apart to stick in both ends of me at the same time!*
>
> —S, 37

●●●

> *Having a threeway with my girlfriend means I get to watch her eat pussy. It's so hot. As a man, I really get into it and so does she.*
>
> —K, 29

Experiment with Adventurous Monogamy

Threeways are also a way to experiment with non-monogamy in an environment that feels safe for all parties. If you are an established couple, it's a way to explore sex with a new person and try new things but still feel together and connected. It's easy to get stuck in a rut after many years of monogamous sex with the same person. Couples often get lazy and adopt an "if it ain't broke don't fix it" attitude about their sex lives, but secretly feel disappointed. Having a threeway can bring some new tricks to your bed that last even after the third person has headed home. A threeway can be your entry into playing with partners outside your relationship, or it can just be a way to see your partner in a new light. Inviting someone else into your bedroom is sure to switch up your dynamic. You'd be surprised how exciting it can be to suddenly see your lover through a fresh lens. Threeways are a way that curious couples can explore all sorts of new roles and ideas. "You have each other there to watch. You have some protection. When couples play together they can protect each other emotionally and physically in a way that they can't really do while playing separately," says Metis Black, a threeway aficionado and co-owner and president of Tantus Silicone, a company that manufactures high-quality sex toys. "A threeway is like sex toys; it's a new thing to play with, and a new way to have fun in bed."

If your partner wants to open up the relationship to sleeping with others, but you feel reluctant, having a threeway is a way to introduce other players while still maintaining control over the situation.

Staying Single

If you are single and prefer staying that way, sleeping with two people has some definite advantages. It's very difficult to remain in the "just dating" phase with one person. After you've spent some serious time together the relationship starts to progress on its own, in spite of your best intentions to keep from getting seriously involved. There's a natural momentum to a relationship that is hard to fight. Sleeping with an established couple means you can get as involved as you want, but still manage to maintain your singleness. You might find that playing with a couple can help you get more of your needs met because there are two people there to meet them. Many people describe dating or just sleeping with a couple as their optimal sexual experience. As a single person, you get to drop in on someone else's relationship and enjoy the intimacy and love that they've created between them, but remain as independent as you need to.

Same-Sex Experimenting

A threeway is also a great way to experiment with someone of the same gender if you haven't done it before. A lot of otherwise straight folks, both men and women, stated that they felt more comfortable having first-time same-sex experiences when someone of the opposite sex was present. If you are curious but not comfortable having a one-on-one experience then a threeway is the perfect way to go. Some people find that a threeway ends up being a pivotal experience in their sexual orientation, and afterward they want sex exclusively with people of the same gender. Not all threeways are gateway drugs to being gay, though most threeways are mind-opening experiences. If you really want to play around with someone of your same sex, but you don't know how to break it to your wife, I think you'll find that a threeway is a good excuse.

> *I think my ideal relationship situation is in a long-term threeway. I've dated couples before and I'm usually happier when there are two people around, that way I don't feel neglected when one lover is too busy. And playing with a couple often means I get to be the new girl, the object of adoration by both lovers.*
>
> —S, 28

•••

I actually came out after my first threeway. I was 21. My boyfriend and I slept with my best friend. I went down on her and something just clicked. All I could think was "I want to do this all the time."

—D, 36

•••

I knew I was a dyke for years before I actually came out. It wasn't that I was afraid to come out, it was just that I really loved my boyfriend as a person and didn't want to leave him. We had threeways as a way of letting me have lesbian sex without leaving the relationship. Eventually we broke up, but for years threeways kept us together.

—B, 39

Let Go of Your Hang-Ups

We live in a very heterocentric, couple-centric, and monogamy-centric society. We're bombarded with messages that tell us pleasure is wrong, sexual experimentation is wrong. But if we bought the messages that get pounded into our heads every day we'd all be having sex once a year in order to produce offspring. Or in other words, we'd all be chumps. Queer or straight, long-term relationships take work and keeping the sex hot should be a big priority. It's perfectly possible to have porn-star sex with your husband or wife if you put a little effort into it. And hopefully this book will show you how.

Sex is my favorite form of recreation. And it's the favorite form of recreation of everyone I get involved with. But I can only do so much pro-sex proselytizing before I start to sound like a horny cheerleader. So let's just assume you've worked through some of your sexual hang-ups or you wouldn't be reading a book on how to have threeways. I'm sure it's tempting to skip ahead to the chapters about how to do it, but if you do you will miss out on lots of fun tidbits from other sexually adventurous folks who've had threeways and lived to tell the tale.

> *Some of the hottest sex I've had has been in threeways. Something happens, everyone involved gets really into the idea that we are having a threeway and the sex just ends up being way over the top.*
>
> —A, 45

•••

> *My favorite threeway was with two guys. I had a cock in my mouth and in my pussy at the same time. Heaven!*
>
> —A, 23

Why Read a Book on Threeways?

Maybe you've been fantasizing about having a threeway for a while now but you've felt weird about taking that first step? Maybe you are in a relationship and want to have a threeway but are afraid to bring it up to your partner? Or maybe you've had a million threeways and you are hoping to learn some new tricks. Regardless of your reason, the purpose of this book is to demonstrate that lots of folks of all persuasions and genders are perfectly willing to get it on with more than one partner at a time. It takes a little work, but what fun thing comes easily. Threeways get a bad rap because of the way they are often portrayed in mainstream porn. But if we used mainstream porn as our only form of sex ed, we'd all be in trouble.

With the right amount of communication and effort there's no reason you can't add a third person to your bed, or become the bologna in a couple sandwich anytime the mood strikes. Lots of folks are doing it. And if you pay close attention, you might just be able to pull it off, too.

What Are You Looking For?

What you are looking for in your threeway is going to affect the kind of experience you have. Let's say you've always wanted to watch your partner with someone else. It's a more common fantasy than you'd imagine. Nearly all of the couples who responded to questions about threeways for this book expressed some desire to see their partner with another person. A threeway is also the perfect way to try out a sexual activity that your usual partner might not dig. Maybe you are normally the more submissive partner in a relationship but you'd like to experiment with being more aggressive or possibly even dominant. Well, your lover might not agree to throwing her legs in the air, but she might be perfectly amenable to watching you take control with someone else.

A threeway is the perfect excuse to plan an elaborate scene. It's small enough to be manageable but having three people instead of two gives you many more options for things like gang-bang fantasies, double penetration, and voyeurism. Adding another body to the mix increases your options. You can watch or show off. You can fuck or get fucked. You can suck or get sucked, or you can do it all at once. A threeway can be an inspiring way to change it up, push your boundaries, or teach you something new.

> *My girlfriend loves to fantasize about me getting fucked by another butch while I'm sucking her cock. It's her favorite jack-off fantasy.*
>
> —S, 26

●●●

●●●

I thought I'd lose my mind if I saw my bisexual girlfriend get fucked by a guy. But in reality it was the hottest thing I'd ever seen. I totally identified with him, even though I'm a dyke, and could practically feel myself fucking her as I watched him fuck her.

—D, 42

POTENTIAL THREEWAY PITFALLS AND HOW TO AVOID THEM

There are a lot of reasons that we might be scared to have a threeway, even though we want one. But most all of them can be dealt with in a rational matter. Threeways are not always problem free, but what is?

FEAR #1: IF I WANT A THREEWAY, I'M A SLUT OR THERE'S SOMETHING WRONG WITH MY CURRENT SEX LIFE.

REALITY: Wanting to have a threeway means you have a sense of sexual adventure and you aren't afraid of trying new things. Does this mean you are a slut? Perhaps, but as someone who simply loves sluts I can't imagine why that's a bad thing. Congratulations. Please go out and buy a copy of *The Ethical Slut* by Dossie Easton and Catherine A. Liszt and commence enjoying yourself.

FEAR #2: IF I WANT A THREEWAY, IT WILL DESTROY MY RELATIONSHIP.

REALITY: Nothing will destroy your relationship if you don't let it. If you and your partner feel secure and you have established good communication, then experimenting with multiple-partner sex can make you closer. Don't do anything the two of you don't agree on. Be open-minded and willing to compromise. Never force your partner to engage in sexual activity he or she isn't comfortable with.

FEAR #3: THE OTHER TWO PARTIES WILL BE MORE ATTRACTED TO EACH OTHER THAN THEY ARE TO ME.

REALITY: While you can't always control something like this, you can definitely make sure you have your head on straight before you enter into any kind of new sexual situation. If you are entering into a threeway with someone you love, it's that person's responsibility to help you feel secure during the scene. And if your self-esteem is intact, and it should be before you have a threeway, then you can handle just about any sexual scenario.

QUEERNESS, LABELS, GENDER

First of all, a threeway doesn't necessarily require a variety of genders and sexual orientations. I'm primarily a lesbian, and the majority of my threeway experiences have been with two other women. The threeways were more about having as much fun as possible rather than experimenting with my sexual identity or challenging myself with new tricks. And one of my gay male friends who routinely finds himself having threeways agrees that it isn't about pushing boundaries or challenging anything, it's just about having fun with more than one body.

That said, sometimes folks who identify as straight want to get it on with a person of the same sex but feel more comfortable doing it with a person of the opposite sex present. It's a way of experimenting without feeling the need to label yourself. One straight man I interviewed routinely plays with gay men but doesn't consider himself gay in any way. "I have a wife and a girlfriend. I'm not gay; it's just sex. Sometimes it's fun to try new things," he explains.

I think straight guys have it rough in our society when it comes to their gender identity. Too many people are concerned with policing the boundaries of masculinity and setting rules about what it means to be masculine enough. One common example of this is a fear that anal play is inherently queer. You know how some straight guys are afraid that if their girlfriend sticks a finger up their ass it means they are gay? Well, unless that finger is actually a penis, and that penis is attached to a guy, and you want that penis all the time and lose interest in the girlfriend, you probably aren't gay. Luckily there are more and more guys out there who've learned to look beyond that sort of limited thinking.

And the same goes for queers. It may seem to the average het that queers have worked out all their issues about labels and identity, but that isn't true at all. Lots of lesbians are curious about playing with boys, and lots of gay boys are curious about pussy but would never go there out of fear of reproach from their peers or worries about what it means to their sexual identity.

In recent years sex parties have risen up in various sexually liberal cities that have embraced the idea that queers of all stripes might want to play with each other. One notorious New York party encourages the gay boys and girls to all play together in the same room. You'd be surprised how resistant queers can be to mixing it up with each other, but luckily a few forward-thinking folks have started a movement away from that kind of limited thinking. Just because you're a homo doesn't mean you can't experiment!

> *My girlfriend and I got approached by one of our gay male friends for a threeway. He wanted us both to fuck him. I was all for it, but my girlfriend got kind of squeamish*

before we could make a date. I'm kind of hoping it might come up again though.

—D, 31

•••

I'm a gay boy but I totally want to get fucked by some big butch daddy dyke with a strap on. I mean I know it's a little weird, but I really think it's hot.

—S, 35

•••

My girlfriend fantasizes all the time about fucking cute gay boys up the ass. It's her favorite thing. She's never done it in real life, but she jerks off to it regularly.

—M, 29

Labels, Schmabels

The truth is, labels are just simple ways to categorize ourselves and each other. But a lot of the time we get caught up in what they mean and become afraid to branch outside of them. Maybe we are afraid of what it means if we have always thought of ourselves as one way and find out that we're actually a whole bunch of ways. Or maybe we are afraid of being judged by our peers. There are a million reasons why we might cling to our labels, but in order to really enjoy a threeway we're going to want to let go of some of them. Threeways have a way of obliterating gender roles and sexual preferences, and opening up our views of ourselves as sexual creatures.

The very act of trying to fit ourselves and each other into boxes like "straight," "gay," or "bisexual" exposes the constructed nature of those boxes. And once you head into threewayville, you are giving up your Moral Majority card anyway. So, may I suggest you do what I like to do? Give the finger to the dominant heterosexist paradigm and invite a bunch of people over to fuck.

In my mind and for the purposes of this book, queer sex is anything that doesn't fit in with the straight procreative sex angle. So in other words, threeways are pretty queer. And if you are interested in taking it that far why not open your mind to the possibility of playing with a gender that's outside your usual choice?

Alternative Relationships

Love, relationships, and monogamy are all wonderful things. But it's a fact that our sexual desires don't always line up with the people we fall in love with. But just because you want to get zipped into a body bag or have your face walked on with stiletto heels and your boyfriend prefers to cuddle while watching ice dancing doesn't mean your relationship doesn't gel. You still love each other. You still have fun sex. And it's perfectly OK to want things that aren't always on the menu at home. It just means that you might need to look outside your bedroom for fulfillment.

Having a threeway can help you add some new things to the menu, it can help couples mix it up a bit and it can help single folk experiment with new tricks. It's like getting to order off the a la carte menu when you've been having the prix fixe.

> *I got what I wanted when I started playing with other boys, and what I wanted was anal sex. I couldn't really convince my girlfriend to fuck me the way I wanted to get fucked no matter how many times we discussed it. But the faggots I started playing with were more than happy to fuck my ass till I was sore.*
>
> —T, 44

●●●

I had my first experience with a boy in a threeway situation. He was gay and had never been with girls. I am a dyke and had never played with boys. And my girlfriend was bi and had done both. She kind of facilitated the whole thing. It was amazing.

—S, 26

•••

One night I found myself having sex with a girl and another guy. I didn't know either of them very well; we were all casual friends. Everyone seemed game and the girl was having a great time. We'd been hanging out together at a party and it was just kind of one of those things that happens with a group of sexually adventurous people. We were in the girl's bedroom, I think her name was A. Anyway, the other guy and I were mostly paying attention to A and not to each other, but I figured what the hell and stroked his cock. I was really turned on by the idea of giving him a blow job. I'd never really had sex with a guy before. I mean I'd fooled around with other boys when I was a teenager, but I think that was more about curiosity about sex than sex with boys in particular. He didn't react well. He pushed my hand away and seemed annoyed. And to this day I think he was being an idiot. I mean, why not? Why shouldn't he and I have had sex with each other and not just with her? Weren't we all naked and having fun?

—H, 34

Sexual Fluidity

Over the course of our lifetimes we change and grow as individuals. It would be bizarre if we were the same person at twenty-four and at forty-four. Yet it's common for people to define their sexual identity in their early twenties and never give it another thought. Our sexuality is mutable just like the rest of us. And over the course of your life you can expect it to take many different shapes. Viewing your sexuality as fluid can be a major step in expanding your sex life. There's no need to explain every time a shift takes place. I can't tell you how many times I've heard statements like: "What? I thought she was a lesbian, how can she sleep with a guy?" or "If you are fooling around with another woman, you must be a dyke."

Even the most open-minded folks get caught up in sexual labels and identity. Labels have their place. I'm not saying we need to do away with them. I'm suggesting we worry less about what they mean. There's no reason we need to police the boundaries of each other's queerness, or straightness, or anythingness. Straight folks aren't going to turn into flaming homos just because they are enjoying a little same-sex action. Gay or straight, it's healthy to let go of some of our sexual rigidity. It makes sex more fun and doesn't make you any more depraved than you already are, you dirty pig, you.

> *My wife and I used to play with another woman regularly. We met her at a mutual friend's dinner party. The friend introduced us, and apparently this other woman—let's call her S—told our friend that she found us attractive as a couple. We'd had threeways before, so it wasn't out of the ordinary, and after meeting a few times for drinks we decided we'd go ahead and make a date for sex. It was so fun that we immediately wanted to do it again the next week.*
>
> *The three of us had an ongoing relationship until S got a serious boyfriend and decided to settle down for a while. It was a great arrangement. We agreed that we could only*

see each other when all three of us were present and that kept the jealousy factor to a minimum. Sometimes she and my wife would have sex while I watched, sometimes we'd all roll around together. The fact that we were already a threeway and therefore somewhat experimental freed us from a lot of our straight, vanilla conventions and on more than one occasion I found myself doing stuff I'd never imagined I'd get into.

For instance, S was bisexual and had penetrated her lovers with a strap-on many times. One night she brought her strap-on over and she and my wife took turns fucking each other with it while I jerked off. Afterward, my wife said she'd always fantasized about fucking my ass with a dildo. I was nervous, but I couldn't deny being turned on by the idea. S coached her and with a lot of patience and lube she managed to fuck me until we both came. It was incredibly hot. The next day at work I couldn't stop thinking about it. I kept looking around at all the other married guys and thinking what suckers they were, having boring married lives, maybe getting laid once a month when I was having the best sex of my life practically every night.

—D, 43

Now that we've discussed all sorts of reasons why we might want to have a threeway it's time to move on to the next chapter where we will learn how to discuss a threeway with our partner, how to make our threeway fun for everyone, and how to make sure our relationships—whether they are casual or long-term—are healthy and strong enough to make a threeway work.

CHAPTER 2

DATING, MATING, RELATING

IT'S TIME TO EMBARK on the fun yet possibly complicated process of making sure your threeway goes down smoothly. Throwing a threeway is a little more tricky than just climbing in bed with the neighbors. If you are coupled up you need to plan your experience with your partner so that both of you are prepared mentally for the consequences of opening up your love nest. And if you are single you'll want to make sure that your threeway, like any other sexual experience you have, is something positive that makes you feel good about yourself. We have sex for lots of reasons other than simple physical gratification, and taking a good long look at those reasons can teach you a lot about yourself. Sex should always make you feel happy and desirable. In this chapter we'll talk about the different forms a threeway can take. We'll also talk about sexual communication, self-esteem, boundaries, and expectations. I'm sure you want to get to the part where I tell you how to get Pamela Anderson or maybe Anderson Cooper to come over and party. But you need this stuff, too, really.

BASIC THREEWAY STRUCTURES

Your threeway is probably going to follow one of three basic models.

1. THE THREE OF YOU MET SIMULTANEOUSLY AND DECIDED TO HAVE SEX. Maybe you were all friends, or

you just picked each other up at the bus stop, or maybe you hooked up during a sex party. The point is, the relationship between the three of you is equal at all points. There are no partner negotiations and no worries that this arrangement is going to affect your ongoing relationship.

2. YOU ARE A COUPLE PLAYING WITH A THIRD. The two of you have a preexisting relationship. This could be any type of relationship, not necessarily a long-term one. Maybe the two of you are just dating or maybe you've been married for ten years. Regardless, the two of you have some sort of bond and have agreed to bring a third party into your sex play because both of you find it exciting.

3. YOU ARE SINGLE AND INTO A COUPLE. A lot of single people find that playing with a couple is very satisfying. In some cases it's because you—the single person—find your life is too busy for a one-on-one relationship, and playing with a couple is a good sexual outlet for you but keeps you from getting involved in an ongoing relationship. Or it could be that playing with a couple offers a certain type of variety you can't get with just one person. For instance, bisexual men and women often find that playing with a male/female couple offers the best of both worlds.

The Free-for-All Threeway

If your threeway falls into the first category there's a lot less to negotiate beforehand. In fact most of the work will be centered around making sure you feel good about yourself. Any group of three is subject to imbalances, I mean just look at *Survivor*, and those kids aren't even sleeping with each other. Well, not on camera. It's natural to form alliances, but this doesn't mean anyone should ever feel left out. You could find that two of you are more interested in playing with each other than you are playing with the third person. Or the other two might click on some other plane, like maybe they are both big opera queens and you don't know The Ring Cycle from the spin cycle. Well, that's OK. Hopefully they won't talk Wagner in bed.

To have a successful threeway you'll need to have your self-esteem intact and you'll need to be prepared for just about anything. Whenever we have sex with a new lover we open ourselves up to all sorts of possibilities. And when we're playing with more than one person there are more personalities to navigate and double the risk of complications. There are also double the benefits, however. A threeway offers double the excitement and double the sexual pleasure of a single lover.

> *I met two other guys in a chat room. We all seemed to be hitting it off so we agreed to meet up at a bar. The flirtation was just as hot in person so we went to my place and had really great sex all night. Everyone went home satisfied.*
>
> —D, 27

•••

> *I love having threeways, and fourways. Really, the more the merrier.*
>
> —S, 32

The Couple-Plus-One Threeway

Option two is slightly more involved. If you are half of a couple you need to make extra sure that you and your sweetie know exactly why it is that you want a plaything. Bringing in a new playmate can add all sorts of spice to your love life, and seeing your lover through someone else's eyes can make them seem brand-spanking new all over again. Many couples claim that watching their lover orgasm with another person, or seeing their partner as a sex object through someone else's eyes has rekindled a dying sex life. But it takes work. You'll want to be very clear on why you want to have a threeway. If you are curious about sex outside of your relationship because you are unhappy or are looking for a way out, a threeway is probably not a smart idea.

Threeways are exciting when your relationship is healthy and stable. But if things aren't running smoothly, involving another person can cause all sorts of drama, insecurity, and jealousy. Be clear on your expectations. Sex educator and *Playgirl* columnist Jamye Waxman advises couples to be very clear on their physical boundaries before participating in a threeway. "It's a good idea to have some signals or maybe a safe word so that couples can check in with each other during their threeway. That way if something goes farther than either partner is comfortable with there is a way to stop the action without having to stop the entire event."

> *The threeway we had was great, but I was kind of unprepared to watch my boyfriend go down on another girl. I think if we did it again, I'd want to reserve certain sexual activities as relationship only.*
>
> —D, 28

•••

> *I'm a woman who had a threeway with my boyfriend and his best friend. It was fun and we all spent the night together afterward. But a few weeks later the two of them had a falling out and I really think it was connected to our threeway. I think my boyfriend wasn't happy with some of the things that went down but he didn't want to admit it.*
>
> —K, 32

The Free to-Be-Me Threeway

Option three is a great way to experiment with multiple-partner sex without worrying about how the dynamics will pan out. You have a lot more control as a single person hooking up with a couple. Most of the boundary negotiation is the responsibility of the couple; your job is to be an object of desire. "I loved being the object of desire of two people who loved each other," says Waxman. Hooking up with a couple can be a great way to experiment and learn a few things about your turn-ons. And it can be a good introduction to playing with the same sex. Waxman explains, "I wanted to experiment more with women, but I wasn't interested in gay bars because I didn't actually identify as gay. I kind of wanted to have the option of just figuring it out without having to label myself. I went into my first threesome worrying that the other woman would feel left out, but it turned out I enjoyed being with her more than him."

> *I like being single and being able to drop in to someone else's relationship once in a while.*
>
> —S, 38

TALKING ABOUT YOUR FANTASIES

So, you are one half of a horny couple. You've thought it through and you have no hidden agendas. It isn't about altering or ending your relationship. You are convinced a threeway is going to rock your socks off. All that's left to do is clear it with the significant other. There are many ways to approach this but whatever route you take your first priority should be making sure your partner feels secure. Now is probably a good time to assure your partner that you want to be with him or her no matter what.

Discussing change and introducing another person to your private-couple sex life can be a really intimidating thing to do. But look at the payoff! You'll add variety, learn to experiment, discover things about your self and your lover, and you'll grow together.

All of this makes for a better, stronger, and happier relationship.

Waxman advises couples to broach the topic when you are both in a relaxed and sexy mood. "It's easier to open the discussion if you approach it as pure fantasy. You can ask your lover if he or she has ever thought about having a threeway and whether or not they find the idea hot. If you've had a threeway in previous relationships, find a way to discuss your sexual backgrounds that seems normal and nonthreatening. Describe a threeway fantasy or read an erotic story to your lover that contains a hot threeway scene. Don't make it into a big thing. Avoid making it seem essential. You want your partner to feel comfortable engaging with the idea for his or her own sake, not just because they feel like they need to please you."

One obstacle to talking with our lovers about our desires is our fear of rejection. "The first thing that goes through my mind when I want to try something new is a fear my partner will think I'm weird," says a forty-two-year-old male whose wife has run home pleasure-parties for the past four years. "It's not that [my wife] has ever been judgmental around sex, she's always been really easy to talk to. And now with her pleasure-party business talking about sex is what she does for a living. But it's difficult to get around the lessons we're taught as kids. I grew up thinking that women didn't like sex as much as men and that if I wanted something besides very straightforward married sex that I was sick or perverted and should hide that desire so no one would know. Then I met [my wife] and she loved sex. She loved talking about it and trying new things. We've been together for six years and our sex life is really hot. But we are definitely still learning from each other."

Rachel Kramer Bussel, *Village Voice* sex columnist and senior sditor at *Penthouse Variations*, points out that it's easier to bring up a new idea if you already have an established open dialogue around sex. "Of course you are going to fear rejection if you and your partner have never discussed your sex life openly. Without that kind of communication you don't really have any idea of what your partner's reaction might be. Couples should learn to talk about sex as naturally as anything else in their relationship. If it's not easy for you, start small. Bring up something from your sexual history. Or, over breakfast, mention something that happened the night before. Once you've made sex a normal part of your daily conversation it won't seem nearly as frightening to ask for something new."

> *My wife and I talk about sex all the time. It's totally natural to us. We often send each other sexy e-mails during the day.*
>
> —D, 37

Fear of Offending Our Lovers

Another obstacle to effective sexual communication is fear of offending our lovers. I myself am struck by this all the time. It's not uncommon to worry about hurting our lover's ego by suggesting a change in routine. The trick is to present the new idea in a way that doesn't make it seem as if what you were already doing wasn't good enough. The easiest way around this kind of worry is to have an ongoing dialogue about sex with your partner so that he or she doesn't feel blindsided when you suddenly want to try out a new type of sex.

Bringing up your desire for a threeway can be a little nerve-wracking. It's easy to worry that your partner will think that he or she isn't doing enough to please you. Get around this by being very clear with yourself about why you want to try a particular activity and how exciting it feels to have your lover join you.

> *The first time I used a vibrator with my boyfriend he got pissed off. He thought I was saying that he couldn't get me off. But we talked about it and I explained that I, as a woman, liked the vibrator as an addition to his mouth,*

fingers, and cock. He stopped seeing it as an insult and more as a new tool to have fun with.

—C, 24

RULES OF GOOD COMMUNICATION

While it's OK to test drive new ideas and figure things out along the way, there are still some ground rules that will make communicating about sex easier. You will probably come up with a set of your own that fits your personality and your relationship but starting out with a set of basics can make it less intimidating. You never really know how your partner feels about something until it gets brought up. Don't assume your lover is a mind reader.

10 Basic Rules of Sexual Communication:

1. TIME AND PLACE. Talk about sex when you are both relaxed and happy. Don't bring up sex during a fight unless you never want to have sex again.

2. REALLY LISTEN TO YOUR PARTNER. Listening is different than just hearing all the words he or she is saying. Don't react before he or she is finished. Don't talk over him or her. Don't bully. Avoid being judgmental. Let your lover speak her mind.

3. RELAX. It's just sex. It's not brain surgery. No one's life is at stake. Try to enjoy talking about sex as much as you enjoy having sex.

4. START SLOWLY. Baby steps are good. If you feel like a threeway might be jumping right into the deep end of the pool, start by suggesting the two of you visit a strip club together. Treat your partner to a lap dance.

5. COMPROMISE. Allow your partner to counter with suggestions of his or her own. Meet in the middle. Learn to stand up for what you want without bullying. And open your mind to things you might not have thought of before.

6. DON'T CRITICIZE. Ever. Avoid criticizing your partner at all costs. Feeling criticized will cause your partner to resent you. It's a sure way to ruin a sex life.

7. MAKE IT FUN. Make a game out of it. One couple suggested playing cards and betting with nights of fantasy fulfillment. Whoever wins gets a night of whatever they want.

8. FOLLOW UP. If you do bring something new into the relationship, whether it's a third person or a new toy, follow up after and discuss how it felt. Was it exciting? Talk openly about it.

9. BE SPECIFIC. If you want something in particular, say so. You'll never know how your sweetie feels about a threeway until you ask him or her specifically.

10. BE GLAD FOR WHAT YOU HAVE. Take stock of your current relationship. Express to your partner how lucky you feel to have him or her and how much you appreciate the sex life the two of you have created.

The Language of Desire

If you can't talk about sex, how can you think about it? Language is merely a system of symbols that our brains use to identify things. If you have no language around sex you have no real way to think about sex, even in your own head. So many of our sexual problems could be solved if we taught ourselves and our lovers a way to think and talk about sex that felt expansive and fun rather than degrading or clinical. Have conversations about sex regularly. Make it a part of your daily routine. Agree on a language with your partner. You don't have to say cock, cunt, and fuck if those words turn you off. But you don't have to say penis and vagina either. Be aware of the power of the words you choose. Different people will have their own associations for different vocabulary words.

Words Are Loaded

I've always felt most comfortable with the word cock to describe my girlfriend's dildo; it seemed like a natural fit, not too clinical and somehow less male than dick. I'd never thought about it twice until the day I got feedback from a more-than-slightly neurotic woman in my creative writing workshop. She wrote a page-long essay on the word "cock" in which she explained in very graphic detail that she's uncomfortable with the word "cock" because it makes her think of giant, throbbing, angry purple erections and she didn't want to have to think about those.

After I finished laughing, it occurred to me that she had a point. My associations with that word were completely different from hers. And though it didn't matter so much in that particular setting, it could matter a lot in an intimate discussion. Since that time I've learned to pay attention to the type of language my partners use when talking about sex. If someone refers to their genitals as "down there" you probably don't want to talk about gaping fuck holes with that particular person even if it turns you on to say it. Language is loaded, and according to a lot of theorists it's also biased. It's pretty difficult to talk about female sexual desire using a language that defaults to the masculine and sets the feminine as "other." But being aware of the way we use the symbols and signs of sexuality can really help us communicate more effectively. Find a sexual language that feels natural and teach yourself to use it.

NEGOTIATING BOUNDARIES

Discussing your threeway fantasy with your lover could potentially bring up many new discussion points. One thing to keep in mind is that everything is negotiable, or at least it should be.

> *My boyfriend wanted to have a threeway with my best friend, another woman. At first I was appalled. Then I realized it wasn't the threeway I objected to, it was the best-friend angle. I talked to him about how he'd feel if I wanted to have sex with his best friend and he realized why I was offended. In the end we had a threeway with a girl from school whom both of us barely knew. It was fun. I'd totally do it again.*
>
> —K, 24

If you suggest something to your lover and meet with total resistance, you don't have a lot of options. It's not fair to insist on something if it makes someone you love uncomfortable. And it's bad, bad, bad to make your partner feel like he or she needs to do something they don't want to do in order to keep the relationship going. That's a form of emotional blackmail, and it sucks.

If you are in a relatively new relationship it's better to wait until you are more established as a couple before pushing the issue. The more secure you feel the easier it will be to mix it up. Many times we resist new things because we feel threatened by them, when we might actually be inclined to agree if we felt safe. As the pro-threeway partner it's your responsibility to be honest about the reasons you are curious about the activity. Explain to your partner why you are specifically interested in a threeway. And keep in mind that there are always ways to compromise. Evaluate how important certain parts of your ideal threeway are to you. It's better to give up certain aspects of your fantasy threeway than it is to jeopardize your relationship.

> *My current lover wanted a monogamous relationship when we first started seeing each other. I agreed that we could try it out for a few months and renegotiate once we got more comfortable with each other. She agreed, and six months later she understood how committed I was to making it work with her. She decided she'd be OK with non-monogamy. She's actually the one with two lovers now, and I am only seeing her. It seems to be working out very well.*
>
> —A, 36

Getting Over Stereotypes

If you are interested in trying something new but fear the ways it might change things, or if your lover is interested in trying something and you feel opposed to it—try talking together about it. Bring up the things you fear may happen. Talking about your fears might help lessen them. And sometimes just airing something can make it disappear completely. Discussing your worries with your partner might help to break down some of your stereotypes. One woman stated that she was afraid of proposing a threeway for fear her partner would think she was a slut. It was only after they discussed her fears at length that she realized she was operating on long-held beliefs left over from her adolescence. Once she aired her concerns she was able to let them go. Try to always be clear about what you need. Don't hold back, it will only lead to resentment later. Never agree to do something merely to keep your lover happy.

What Are Your Boundaries?

"You can fake a lot of things," says Bussel. "But you can't fake a threeway. If you are seriously opposed to it, make your feelings known. If you are game to give it a try and you aren't sure how you are going to react, be honest with your partner about that. Tell him or her you'd like to play certain things by ear. And retain the right to stop the action if you feel uncomfortable."

If you've never had any of your boundaries tested, it's possible you don't really know what they are. I've had this come up from time to time in my dating life. Usually it happens when I'm with someone I've just started seeing and it turns out that my version of normal and her version of normal are a little different. Ask yourself the following questions. The answers can help you better understand your needs.

1. ARE THERE ANY sex acts that you have tried and didn't enjoy?

2. WHAT WAS IT that made the situation unpleasant?

3. HAVE YOU EVER been in a situation that made you feel unsafe?

4. IF YOU HAVE FELT UNSAFE, either emotionally or physically, was there something the person you were with could have done to ease the situation?

5. HAVE YOU EVER wanted to talk about something but felt afraid to do so? Why?

6. HAVE YOU EVER felt like you needed to agree to something in order to keep your partner happy?

7. IS THERE SOMETHING your partner did or said that made you feel like you had to agree?

8. HAVE YOU EVER felt surprisingly at ease during a difficult conversation? What made the conversation work?

9. ARE YOU ALWAYS honest with yourself?

10. WHAT SITUATIONS or conversations have triggered jealousy and insecurity in the past?

Just Between Us

Couples might want to agree to designate certain activities as couples only. For instance, kissing or oral sex can be designated a couple only activity, and everything else is considered fair game in a threeway situation. Perhaps you'd prefer it if the third person didn't spend the night? Or maybe certain words and nicknames are designated relationship only. These are things to discuss beforehand, not during. Be prepared, work through possible scenarios in your head before you jump into bed. "I once stopped a threeway while it was happening. I wasn't prepared to watch my boyfriend have sex with someone else. And I put a stop to the action because I knew if I didn't I'd end up resenting everyone. I wanted to stop it before it got to that point," says Waxman. Claiming space for your relationship can help you avoid hurt feelings in the end.

Who's Behind Door Number Three?

Who is this mystery third person anyway? "It's possible you might end up in bed with someone who already knows one of you. That could potentially be more difficult depending on your relationship to the person. Not that you necessarily want to have sex with a stranger, but having sex with your boyfriend's best buddy might cause problems," advises Bussel.

Ideally your third party is someone you are both attracted to. I mean, that might seem like an obvious suggestion but you'll find it's harder than you think to agree on your ideal sexbot. Sometimes even in fantasy this mystery third party looks like Harrison Ford in *Star Wars* to one of you and the MILF next door to the other. I've had more than one girlfriend get really into the idea of bringing another gal around until we got down to the actual idea of who it could possibly be. I like to test drive sexual scenarios in fantasy play and dirty talk for a few weeks before you get to the point of no return. It's a nice way to line up your turn-ons and your partner's turn-ons. For instance, I usually go for women with a more masculine gender presentation than myself, but that doesn't mean I can't appreciate a bombshell. But I've found that most of my masculine partners, both male and female, really only want to do it with Drew Barrymore. This is the kind of thing you need to know before you get started on your quest. Whether it's a mutual friend or merely an acquaintance, all parties should be into each other. Don't ever pretend to be more into someone than you really are. It's only going to ruin things for everyone involved.

> *I agreed to a threeway with a guy I was seeing very casually. I met him on craigslist and when he brought up the threeway idea I figured craigslist would be a good place to look for our lucky third. But all the women he scared up were not at all attractive to me. He seemed so desperate to have a threeway with me that he wasn't even concerned with who the other woman was. After he made me meet a couple of women who I really thought were, well, skanky, I broke up with him.*
>
> —S, 29

If you go the mutual friend route, choose someone you both feel comfortable with and who feels comfortable with both of you. Close friends don't always make good lovers, although it certainly can be done. One advantage of getting it on with a close friend is that the intimacy you already share can make sex more loving and special. But think it through before you go there. How will you feel watching your lover and your best friend have sex? If you have trepidations, you may want to reconsider.

Regardless of who you choose, make sure you talk with the third party beforehand about what his or her role is. While I'm not suggesting you ask anyone to follow a script, there are a few things that you might want to discuss before you get down. If he or she is expected to go home at the end of the night, make that known before you get started, in order to avoid an uncomfortable situation.

THREEWAY ETIQUETTE

There are no rules, so you'll have to create your own.

Regardless of who your third party ends up being (we'll discuss ways to choose a third partner in Chapter 3), it's important that everyone involved gets treated with respect and affection. If someone feels like a third wheel in your threeway it will pretty much ruin the point of having one in the first place.

While you can't actually control everyone's level of arousal and engagement, you can be polite to all parties involved. No matter what type of threeway you've found yourself in it's important to keep in mind that all three of you are coming from a place of vulnerability. A third person who has joined a couple could be worried about feeling left out, or might be so cautious about overstepping boundaries that he or she in effect makes herself feel left out. One half of a couple might be terrified that his or her partner is going to find the third person more desirable. And any member of a randomly organized triad might worry that the other two will be more attracted to each other than they are to him or her.

> *I was sure my girlfriend was more into the other girl we were with. I was watching them have sex and thinking that I should just leave the room. We talked about it after and my girlfriend was horrified to find out I'd felt so left out.*
>
> —N, 26

Just because you're naked doesn't mean you should all jump around like a bunch of Samsonite gorillas. It's just as important to have good manners during sex as it is to have them anywhere else. Anything that applies to two-person sex also applies to three-person sex. On top of that, there are a few things to keep in mind that are specific to your threeway romp.

1. DON'T FORGET THERE ARE THREE OF YOU. Check in with all parties every once in a while; do whatever it takes to make sure everyone is getting the kind of attention they want. If one person seems left out bring them in; touch them, kiss them, say something lewd. It may be that they enjoy watching the other two parties get busy and are taking a break but it never hurts to make sure.

2. DON'T PUSH. Everyone gets to choose his or her own comfort level. There are three of you; this means there are three different sets of tastes and preferences. While being introduced to new things during sex can be very hot, being pushy about it can be a turnoff.

3. PAY ATTENTION. Don't lose yourself in one activity. There are a lot more parts involved in a threeway than single-partner sex, and if you pay attention to what's

going on you will be able to better navigate the extra arms and legs. Don't get greedy with one person. Be a good sport.

4. RELAX AND TAKE A BREAK FROM TIME TO TIME. Sometimes people just need a rest. You can take breaks all together, or one of you can lie back and watch the other two go at it.

5. HAVE A SENSE OF HUMOR. Sex is funny. It looks weird. It sounds odd. People look funny when they are having sex. Don't get freaked out and feel weird. Funny things happen. It's OK to laugh.

6. MAKE EVERYONE FEEL SPECIAL. Give compliments. Say dirty, nasty, hot things. Get everyone riled up.

7. DON'T DIRECT THE ACTION. You aren't Francis Ford Coppola, you aren't even Sofia Coppola. Don't boss anyone around. And do not, under any circumstances criticize anyone's techniques or behavior.

8. THIS REALLY SHOULDN'T HAVE TO BE SAID, but I'll say it anyway. Be nice to the people you are having sex with.

So now you've learned all sorts of new ways to think and talk about sex. In the next chapter we'll figure out how to find some stranger so you can test drive your new skills.

CHAPTER 3

THE SEARCH IS HALF THE FUN

NOW THAT YOU ARE a communication superhero you'll want to go out and gather up your court of lovers. If you are a couple you'll want to find your ideal third. And if you are flying solo this chapter will give you some suggestions for hooking up with a twosome. There are lots of options for meeting folks—don't worry, I promise you won't have to go on elimiDATE.

YOUR IDEAL LOVER CHECKLIST

Finding a partner or partners for your threeway is similar to finding a partner for couple sex. You'll need to figure out who you are and who you're looking for. Then you want to think about who might be looking for you, and where to find this person.

Start by making yourself a list of the traits you hope to find in your potential third party. Really make a list. Get out a pen and paper. This is an important step. Some of the traits you'll write down should be very basic and specific. What is this person's gender, sexual orientation, and age range? Some traits will be a lot more theoretical. For instance, you should decide if your potential partner needs to be open to something ongoing or long-term. You might want to decide how intimate you'd like to get with them; do they just come over for sex and then leave? Do you have meals together? Is it going to be like *Last Tango in Paris* where you meet for weeks without exchanging names? You also should decide whether or not you'd like to partner up with someone you already know or you prefer fresh meat.

Narrowing Down the Options

If your "who I want to meet" specifications are essentially "anyone with a pulse" you might consider breaking it down a bit. Not that I'm advocating a laundry list of requirements, because of course people that fall into that trap never get laid. But the more you know about the person you are looking for the easier it will be to recognize that person when he or she comes along. If you have strong preferences about body type and other physical attributes it's perfectly fine to acknowledge that. It's OK to want to be with someone you are physically attracted to and some of us have a wider range of what floats our boat than others.

Having Realistic Expectations

However, if you've been watching too much porn and you're basically not interested in having sex with anyone besides Jenna Jameson, good luck with that. I expect you'll be sitting home alone quite a bit. Expecting a lover to achieve unreasonable standards really only sets you up for a lifetime of disappointment and frustration. Attraction is a complex thing and extends way beyond physical appearance. Figuring this out is one of the first steps to having a fantastic sex life.

> *I'm attracted to great lovers. Sometimes they fit a mainstream standard of beauty and sometimes they don't. What really gets me hot is confidence and skill.*
>
> —L, 48

THE SEARCH BEGINS

The search for your ideal third will depend a lot on what type of couple you are. Two gay boys looking for a third will find cruising a lot less complicated than a male-female couple looking for a bi woman or man, simply because gay men have a pretty straightforward approach to cruising and lots and lots of outlets.

Finding a threeway isn't all that different from finding any other kind of lover. You can expect all the same components to be involved. You'll wonder how to attract people, you'll feel insecure from time to time, maybe get rejected. You might attract people you aren't interested in and have to learn polite ways to say no. Your boundaries will get tested, and you'll probably learn some things about yourself.

So, where can you find sex partners? Well just about everywhere, really. Make yourself available. Open your mind. Own your desire to meet someone new. Don't be ashamed or reluctant about your desire for sexual adventure. Searching for a new lover is exciting, so go ahead and get excited. Get yourself turned on by the idea. When you feel confident and sexy, it shows and people will be drawn to it.

You want to meet someone who shares your interests to a certain extent, even if that interest is simply to get it on. Does your city have any sexy events going on? What about erotic art shows or readings? Maybe a workshop? Is there a sex-positive community you can join? What about taking a class? New lovers can be found anywhere. Meeting someone new is usually just a matter of putting yourself out there. There may be a totally hot potential waiting for you, but he or she isn't going to magically show up in your living room.

A FEW POINTERS FOR FINDING A NEW LOVER:

- Know yourself and what you are looking for.
- Break out of your routine. Go places you wouldn't normally go. If you want sexual adventure, you need to have an adventurous lifestyle.

- Get involved in your community. Make friends with people who care about the same things you do. Go to community events.
- Go public. Put the word out. Talk to your friends about your desire to meet someone new.
- Learn to talk about sex and desire. Basic communication skills will take you farther than anything else.

•••

I met two other women at a coffee shop. It was crowded and I asked if I could share their table. It turned out they were together. I wasn't cruising them on purpose, but I always feel like you never know what could happen. We spent the afternoon flirting and exchanged numbers before we headed separate ways.

—T, 32

LEARN TO FLIRT

There he is across the room. It's Fabio, the stud of your dreams. His long blond locks are being blown back by a gentle breeze. He's deeply tanned and he has that weird European accent. Your knees go weak. Your heart beats a little faster. You want him.

But how do you approach him? Flirting comes naturally to some of us; we flirt when we're talking to the customer service people selling us cell phone contracts. We flirt our way through the day using our sexual energy as a social lubricant. But the rest of us might have a little trouble in that department. We might be plenty confident when we have the attention of a lover but getting that attention initially is sometimes intimidating. Well, don't despair, even though there's no surefire way to pick someone up there are a few tricks you can learn that will significantly raise your chances of getting noticed.

1. CONFIDENCE IS SEXY. Don't underestimate the signals you send out through body language and the way you present yourself. You want to be desired, so act desirable. Dress sexy. Practice good grooming. Smile. Like yourself. Pay attention to your posture and have open body language. Crossed arms are intimidating and tell the other person to back off. But leaning in toward someone when they speak lets them know you are interested.

2. MAKE EYE CONTACT. A nice long approving gaze and a smile makes the other person feel desirable. Don't stare at the person like you're a carnivore and he's a wounded antelope hanging out at the oasis—but holding eye contact for a beat or two longer than expected is seductive and sexy.

3. COMPLIMENT THE OBJECT OF YOUR DESIRE, BUT DO SO APPROPRIATELY! "I find you very attractive" is good. "You have really big tits" is bad.

4. LISTEN CLOSELY AND PAY ATTENTION TO HIM OR HER AS SHE SPEAKS. Reference things brought up earlier in the conversation. Your potential trick will be flattered and impressed that you are paying such good attention.

CRUISING AS A COUPLE OR SINGLE

Village Voice sex columnist Rachel Bussel has this advice for a couple looking to meet a third. "I'm constantly seeing cute couples who I'd love to join for a night. It's hard to tell sometimes if a couple is flirting with me, because it's not what I'd normally expect. (Hint: Be direct and explicit if you're trying to pick up a third for your conjugal bed.) As a single person, I can relax and enjoy myself and not worry about any potential relationship drama."

Cruising together as a couple can be a hot way to spend an evening together. Tag-team flirting can get the two of you so turned on you'll appear sexy and attractive to people around you.

Whether you are two girls, two guys, or a guy and a girl, going out together allows you to flaunt your sexiness as a twosome. Flirt with each other. Get off on your partner and you'll find that you attract attention. If you are really attracted to each other, it shows and it makes other people attracted to you. Don't be shy about public displays of affection. I'm not suggesting you throw your date down on the pool table and fuck his or her brains out. And don't be creepy and predatory either. But genuine affection like holding hands, touching, and kissing show the world that you like each other, and that will make people like you. There's something really appealing about a sexy, adventurous couple. People want to be part of it and share in the fun.

A lot of successful sex and romance is about changing your mindset. It's hard to say exactly when a healthy preference or desire becomes an unhealthy obsession, but there's definitely a line that can be crossed. If you are obsessed with the idea of finding a threeway, to the extent that the threeway itself is more important than who you partner up with, your desperation will show and it will turn off any potential romantic interests.

"Much as I'm a threesome fan, the gung-ho guys who are obsessed with threesomes turn me off, making me feel like a pawn in their game. In their rush to eroticize two women getting it on with them, they dehumanize the women. Maybe if they chilled out and let things develop naturally, they'd get their threesome wish fulfilled. Trying to micromanage or force the act makes everyone feel uncomfortable," says Bussel.

Another tip for would-be adventurous couples is to actually talk to a potential date together, as a team. When one of you comes on strong your potential third party might wonder if there's an imbalance of interest in the threeway. "I was approached by a guy at a party. He said 'My girlfriend likes girls, would you be interested in getting together with us?' and I wished that she had approached me instead. His aggressiveness made me suspicious and I wondered if she was interested, or if he was trying to force something," says Jamye Waxman.

Women have some advantages when it comes to flirting with other women. It's less taboo for straight gals to make out with each other. I mean, do you even know any woman who hasn't tossed back a few beers at a party and started snogging her best friend? Also, chicks have access to places and situations that men don't have. I remember being at a friend's baby shower and thinking the attendees should all stop complaining about their sex lives and start sleeping with each other, or even just sleeping with me. I would have probably suggested it, but they seemed like a pretty sexually conservative crowd. I'd brought what I normally bring to showers and bachelorette parties as a gift: a rabbit pearl vibrator. But it didn't go over very well. No one told me I was supposed to bring a stick blender. I blame my mom.

But just because I had bad luck doesn't mean you will. All-female environments can be very sexually charged. If you are female and have never slept with a woman before, I think one of the first things you will realize is that flirting with the ladies is a bit more complicated than with men. OK, for the most part, flirting with straight guys pretty much consists of making yourself available and then letting them do the rest. Sorry guys, but you know it's true. But women are tricky. You will have to be much more direct so that your attention doesn't get misconstrued as simple friendliness. Chicks like to be chased. If you are used to being chased too, you are going to have to step outside that role for a change. If you've never been in the aggressive role before, don't panic. Just think about the ways you've been romanced in your lifetime. Channel them and hone them to fit your current situation. Chances are good you'll love being the aggressor.

If you are a straight gal with a little jones for another gal but you don't know how to approach her, think about what works on you and go from there. Do you like being flattered? Tell her she's hot. Do you think eye contact is sexy? What about feeling objectified? It might not be totally fair, but you'll find that women can get away with saying things to each other that men would get slapped for. Compliment her body. Tell her she has an amazing ass. If she doesn't respond, perhaps she's not interested in playing with girls. Don't worry, there are always more women to flirt with.

Some straight-gal interviewees expressed a fear of flirting with lesbians because they didn't want to be seen as amateurs or as fickle. They wanted their sexual desires to be taken seriously and they worried that they would face biphobia from the lesbian community. Well, it can happen—certainly any group has their share of biases and prejudices. But if you encounter some sort of prejudice that just means that person is not someone you want to go to bed with. Deal with the rejection and move on.

Another benefit to initiating the threeway as the straight-gal half of a couple is the other woman (if that's what you want) is going to feel much more comfortable if she knows right away that it's not all the boyfriend's idea.

> *I'm a man and I met a couple at an art show. They were very attractive and I just started talking to them about the paintings and random stuff. We all found ourselves drawn to each other and I suggested we go get a drink. We went home together that night.*
>
> —B, 30

Lesbian couples looking for some multiple-partner sex will do well at clubs and sex parties. Anywhere you can go and show off what a sexy couple you are is going to be good cruising ground. Dance clubs, crowded bars, the dyke march, Pride parades, women's events, parties, you name it. There are lots of places to find a little threeway action. My ex and I hooked up with one of her exes and it turned out to be a great threeway. I've met girls in coffee shops and bookstores, I've propositioned friends, and been approached by girls who've wanted to sleep with my girlfriend. If you open your mind to possibilities they begin to present themselves.

And gay boys, I hardly feel like they need advice in this area. Gay men have their own style of cruising, and have developed a language around the search for sex that is pretty easy to read. It's really one of the beautiful things about being a queer if you ask me. As queers, we are forced to think about our sexuality every day because it's really what sets us apart. Those of us who have managed to overcome uptight mainstream society's disapproval get to really enjoy our community's comfort level around sex.

So where do you go if you are a male-female couple looking for a third female? Cruising dyke bars will probably get you laughed at. I'm not saying it doesn't happen. But it's probably not a great place to start out. But that doesn't mean there aren't other great places to go and meet the third party of your dreams.

PLACES TO MEET PEOPLE

- Parties
- Art openings
- Erotic readings
- Sex clubs
- The laundromat
- The gym
- The office
- Bookstores
- Libraries

- Museums
- Cafes
- Coffee shops
- Poetry readings
- Bars
- Book clubs
- Classes
- Workshops
- Shopping, especially for sex toys
- The park
- The mall
- Mass transit

One Couple's Success Story

More than one couple I interviewed said that they'd had a great deal of success in hotel bars. And this held true no matter what the gender makeup of the couple was. One couple in particular told me a great story about their hotel hook-up success and explained that hotel bars were a great place to meet women or men who were traveling on business and were open to the idea of being sexually adventurous while they were away. For privacy's sake, let's call these two Brad and Anjolina, shall we? Brad is thirty-four and Anjolina is thirty-six. They live in the Bay Area. They have been married four years and have no kids. They are an adventurously monogamous couple meaning they only fool around with other people when they are both present and they like to have sexual adventures as often as possible. They occasionally attend sex parties together and like to have threeways with both men and women.

> *"One of the things that made me fall for Brad was his sense of adventure and the way he would get excited about sex. When we first met we had these marathon sex sessions and I really wanted that initial attraction to last. We both have*

really high sex drives and he's really good at keeping the sex hot. It's been four years and it's even better than it was when we first met," says Anjolina.

"Anjolina likes sex in hotels anyway, so every once in a while we'll rent a room at a big hotel and stay in and order room service and treat it like a mini sex vacation. She'll pack a bunch of sex toys and we'll talk to each other about it all week long and get kind of worked up about all the sex we're going to have," says Brad.

"Well the second time we took our mini hotel vacation we had a few drinks in the bar and I saw this really good looking woman who was by herself and I bought her a drink. I wasn't consciously hitting on her. At the time I just thought I was having fun and being bold. But she responded really well and the three of us had a great conversation. At the end of the night we invited her to come upstairs with us and she accepted," says Anjolina.

"It wasn't our first threeway, but it was our first threeway with someone we didn't know very well. And it was great. Both women were totally hot and into each other. The other woman turned out to be really sexually aggressive and bisexual, which was kind of a nice thing because a few other times we've been in bed with another woman and she just sort of lay there expecting to be adored. The three of us had a lot of fun that night," says Brad.

"We tried that same bar again a few months later and met someone that night too. It wasn't quite as fun as the first time, but still it was an interesting evening. And the thing is, even if we don't meet someone we still have great sex in

a hotel room with each other and someone else has to wash all the sheets and towels," says Anjolina.

●●●

Sex and the Single Guy or Gal

Many single people like the idea of dating and sleeping with a couple. For the bi or bi curious, it's a sure route to the best of both worlds. But where do you find adventurous couples? My friend C is a pretty experienced threeway player and her advice is to be vocal about your desires. If you are looking for a threeway, let people around you know. "When I'm with someone, I'm upfront with him or her about wanting to hook up with a third person. And it's always in the back of my mind when we are out," says C.

So what about cruising for a couple when you are on your own? You can always turn to the Internet, proposition your friends, or head for a swingers party, and we will get into all those scenarios later in this chapter. But if you happen to be out in public and you run into Electra Woman and Dyna Girl and you simply must follow them home, then there are ways to bring it up without seeming pushy.

If you find yourself flirting with one or both halves of a couple while you are out in public you should be able to ascertain pretty quickly whether or not both parties are receptive to your attention. If one partner seems annoyed, back off. But if both parties are engaging you then it's totally possible they are open to the idea of taking you home with them. Try subtly turning the conversation to sex and gauge the reaction. By subtly I mean mention how attracted you are to both of them, don't just blurt it out. Or make it known that you are single and looking. If it goes well, loosen up and be a little bolder. Compliment them as a couple. Don't play favorites. And while it's good to be open about your desire, it's best to let the couple take the lead.

A word to the aggressive flirts out there. Don't push yourself on people who aren't interested. It's bad manners. And if you are a straight guy, don't get aggressive with female-female couples. It really makes you seem like a bad stereotype. I'm actually surprised at how often this happens.

Friends and Friends of Friends

It's kind of a cliché, but it's not a tired one. People sleep with their friends. It happens, and a lot of the time it makes a relationship stronger and more intimate. My very first threeway was with my boyfriend and best friend. And we all had a great time. My best friend and I still laugh about it today.

Are you attracted to one of your friends? Do you feel like there's a little spark there that you'd like to develop? I'm not necessarily suggesting you put the moves on your closest confidante. You'll want someone to tell the story to. But acquaintances and folks that fit more peripherally in your life might just be the perfect third wheel on your would-be sex tricycle. I've been seduced by friends of mine with direct propositions and by subtle hints. I've had folks say to me, "You're coming home and having a threeway with us," which is pretty much as clear as it gets. But another approach could be inviting that certain someone to a dinner party and suggesting he or she sticks around after all the guests leave. If there's someone in your life you feel attracted to but your coffee shop dates have remained strictly coffee, try inviting them to something a little sexier. What about getting a massage together? Go dancing. Watch movies together. Go to the gym and sit in the sauna. Half the gay men I know have met hookups in the sauna at the gym—there's no reason it can't work for all the sexes, right?

Play Twister

Another great way to make your friendships a little sexier is to throw a party. Tell your friends to invite their friends and you might meet some new people and potential dates. Ask everyone to invite someone single and looking; make hooking up the theme of the party. Put the word out, let everyone know what you want. Your friends can help you by introducing you to people. Your friends know you, and they know what types of people you'll be attracted to.

Start a game of spin the bottle. Do body shots. Have hickey-giving contests. Get some sexy fun going. Break out of your boring, desperate rut. If you want to have an adventurous sex life you have to create it.

Rejection Happens, Get over It

Sometimes you get turned down. It's OK. It's nothing to feel weird about. With all this looking around going on, you will occasionally find yourself attracted to someone who isn't interested. Or maybe the opposite will happen and someone you aren't interested in will approach you. A simple "no, thank you" is the best way to respond. Keep in mind that a rude rejection reflects poorly on the person doing the rejecting, not the person being rejected. Bad manners are terribly unsexy.

Practice Good Dating Skills

Looking for a lover or lovers can mean opening yourself up to all sorts of new people. While this is going to be lots of fun, it's also important to understand what your own behavior rules are and to learn to judge appropriate behavior in other people. Inviting someone with bad dating behavior into your love life can make things messy.

And getting a really clear picture of your comfort zone is a big step in having an emotionally healthy and gratifying sex life.

QUESTIONS TO ASK YOURSELF:

1. DO I WANT to have sex with this person?
2. AM I ATTRACTED to this person?
3. AM I BEING CLEAR about what I want?
4. AM I GIVING MORE than I am getting?
5. DOES THIS PERSON respect me?
6. DOES THIS PERSON have respect for his or her self?
7. DOES THIS PERSON want more from me than I really want to give?
8. IS THIS PERSON being clear about his or her expectations?
9. IS THIS PERSON getting too close too soon?

CRUISING ONLINE

How on earth did anyone ever meet anyone before the Internet? Especially if you live outside of a major city or in a socially conservative community, the fastest route to getting laid is placing an online ad. If there's an active craigslist.com message board in your city or town, you're halfway to whatever sexual combo meal your little heart desires. The main disadvantage to cruising for tricks online is that the amount of people looking for love on the World Wide Web can be a little overwhelming. You'll need a few ways to narrow down your search. Writing a good ad and carefully stating what you are looking for is a good place to start.

How to Write an Online Personal

Check the Casual Encounters section of craigslist.com and you'll find about a gazillion postings of couples looking for threeways. Read through some of the ads to give yourself an idea of what's out there and what people are looking for. One of the interesting things about online ads is that because people can put up anything they want, the standards are often rather low. Don't be one of those low-standards couples. Hopefully you still have that ideal sex partner checklist you made earlier in the chapter because you will want to refer to it now. Back in the day when people used to place ads in newspapers and other print sources they came up with a bunch of codes to save on word space. But much like the universe, the Internet is infinite and we don't really need those anymore. Think of your ad like a cover letter. It should be brief and to the point and give the reader a good idea of who you are and what you want. And by all means, spell check it before you put it up. Nothing is less sexy than bad spelling.

Examples of Online Ads

I pulled these ads right off the Internet. The first example is unedited. The second example is the same ad with a few added descriptive terms and specifics that make the ad seem more real and appealing. Compare the two and see if you can use these examples to improve your own personals ad.

GOOD AD: "We are two hung horny bi guys looking for a female for threeway fantasy fulfillment. One of us is tall and muscular, the other is short and fit. We're both fun, funny, giving, well educated, professional, and discrete."

IMPROVED AD: "We are two hung horny bi guys looking for an athletic, outgoing female for threeway fantasy fulfillment. One of us is tall and muscular, the other is short and fit. We're both fun, funny, giving, well educated, professional, and discrete. Please be open-minded, witty, and ready for fun."

GOOD AD: "Curious couple seeks BBW for wild threeway fun. We are happily married and sexually adventurous. He's tall, built, blond, and eager to please. She's short, curvy, brown hair, brown eyes, and very busty. We are looking for a one-night thing, with the opportunity to get together in the future if we all enjoy ourselves. We are experienced with this type of arrangement. First-timers welcome."

IMPROVED AD: "Curious couple seeks plus-size sexpot for wild threeway fun. We like our women fine, thick, and proud. We are happily married and sexually adventurous. He's tall, built, blond, and eager to please. She's short, curvy, brown hair, brown eyes, and busty. We are looking for a one-night thing, with the opportunity to get together in the future if we all enjoy ourselves. We are experienced with this type of arrangement. First-timers welcome."

Who Are You?

Start out with a brief description of your relationship status and what you are looking for. If you are a couple mention that upfront. Describe yourselves and your ideal mate. If you are single and trying to meet a couple be very clear about what you want. The number of couples looking for a threeway greatly outnumbers single people looking to hook up. You'll probably get inundated with offers from couples who may not interest you, especially if you are a single female. If you want people to send pictures, make that clear. State in your ad that you plan on only answering responses that interest you. And don't feel like you need to answer every response you get. There are a lot of people out there and you don't want your Internet search to turn into a part-time job, even if you are doing all this while you are at work.

Admit You Like Bergman Films and Country Music

If you want to meet partners that you can also have conversations with, then describe some of your likes and dislikes. Talk a bit about your interests. If you love film, mention some directors that you like. If you are a music snob, name-drop a bunch of hipster indie rock bands. If you like to read, talk about some novels that you love. Be clever, don't be afraid to let your personality show. I met one of my partners through a craigslist ad. I expressed my love for power chords and she sent me the lyrics to a Nelson ballad. When I read her response, little hearts floated out of my eyes.

Online Dating Sites

There are tons of places to fall in lust online. Most dating sites have options for those looking for casual encounters as well as long-term relationships. They all have options for women seeking women and men seeking men, and usually have something set up for couples seeking a third or the other way around. If they don't offer that option explicitly then you will want to make it clear in your profile that you are looking for a threeway. It's incredibly bad manners to lure a single gal into a date and then spring your significant other on her. Lesbians hate that. And if you are a woman seeking a woman and you don't make it clear that you are partnered with a guy, then you definitely don't deserve a threeway. Be upfront about your desires. Trust me on this one.

If you are clear about what you want, and you have reasonable expectations, there's a good chance the Internet will deliver. There are so many places to cruise online I can't even list them all.

Most of these sites work in a similar fashion. You fill out a detailed profile and post pictures of yourself. It usually doesn't cost anything to fill out a profile, but contacting other people on the site will cost you anywhere from four dollars a month to about thirty dollars a month. The main complaints people seem to have about online personals sites is that potential hookups may not always be what they seem in their profile. But this is true in real life as well. Sometimes you meet mister wonderful at a coffee shop and a week later you learn he has three wives. Use good judgment. If someone seems weird, they probably are. And if you like weird, well great. But if you don't then trust your instincts and stay away from the person.

HERE'S A PARTIAL LIST OF ONLINE DATING SERVICES:

Nerve.com
Lavalife.com
Personals.yahoo.com
Match.com
JDate.com
OkCupid.com
AmericanSingles.com
eHarmony.com
Webdate.com
Tickle.com
True.com
Gay.com
Perfectmatch.com
BlackPlanet.com
FriendFinder.com

Sex Services

There are lots of places out in the big world of the Internet specifically designed to get the casual encounter thing going on. One of the more successful ones is AdultFriendFinder.com. Adult FriendFinder is designed a little like Friendster for really horny people. Recently they've added some fantastic content to the site including how-to articles by sex-book authors and adult-film professionals. You pay a small fee to sign up and post a picture of yourself and describe what you are looking for. There's not a lot of small talk here and anything goes. Expect lots of close-up pictures of genitals and be prepared to dig through pages of Internet wankers posing as extremely promiscuous lingerie models. Though overall the site is populated by horny sexual adventurers, if you are serious about finding new sex partners and want to cut to the chase, Adult FriendFinder is the place to go.

Social Networking Sites

Social networking sites are different from dating sites in that they aren't primarily designed for dating, which seems to take the pressure off for users who feel shy about looking for hook ups. Sites like Friendster.com, MySpace.com, and tribe.net work on the premise that you'll get along with your friends' friends better than you will with a total stranger. "Hey, you know Bill, and I know Bill, let's meet for a drink!" When you join you fill out a profile and upload photos of yourself. There are over three hundred social networking Web sites and which one you join is pretty much up to you. Friendster remains one of the most popular places to create online communities.

These sites feature things like automatic address book updates, profiles with pictures, introduction services, and tons of flirting gimmicks and can make meeting new people very easy.

PARTIAL LIST OF SOCIAL NETWORK WEB SITES:

43Things.com—users are connected by similarities in lists they create

DowneLink.com—LGBT community network

Facebook.com—college kids love this one

Faceparty.com—sounds dirty, I know. But it's another college-oriented site

Favorville.com—people helping people

Friendster.com—the oldest and largest of the social sites
GreatestJournal.com—online journaling and community
LinkedIn.com—for the suit set
LiveJournal.com—online journaling and community
MySpace.com—even Paris Hilton has a MySpace profile
Nexopia.com—Canadians like this one
Orkut.com—this is Google's version of the social network
Passado.com—social and business together
Quepasa.com—Latino-oriented network
Slide.com—share your photos and make friends
sms.ac—keep in touch with your mobile phone
tribe.net—another big one like Friendster and Myspace
iWiW.com—invite-only
WAYN.com—travelers
Xanga.com—blogs and networking
XuQa.com—college networking site, similar to Facebook
360.yahoo.com—linked to Yahoo! Ids

SAFETY CONCERNS

When picking up tricks online you should follow the same common sense rules you'd use in any other kind of blind date situation.

1. EXCHANGE A FEW E-MAILS and talk on the phone before you set up your first date. You can glean a lot of information before you meet by having a telephone conversation. If someone insists on meeting right away, be suspicious.

2. DON'T LET YOURSELF GET PUSHED into anything that makes you uncomfortable. If they make demands before you've met, tell him or her that you aren't interested and stop corresponding.

3. **ALWAYS ARRANGE TO MEET** someone for the first time in a public place. Let your friends know where you will be and what time to expect you home.

4. **IF THE PERSON ISN'T** what you expected cut the date short. There's no reason to be rude, but it's perfectly OK to make an exit if you find yourself with someone you aren't attracted to. It's not nice to lead someone on.

5. **GOOGLE THEM.** Google knows all. You can find out ridiculous amounts of information by googling someone's full name. Don't worry, it's not stalking. Googling someone before you meet them is a basic safety precaution.

THE SWINGERS' SCENE

Some hetero couples interested in multiple-partner sex might be attracted to swinging, also known as "the lifestyle" and occasionally referred to as wife-swapping. The deal with swinging according to most of the information out there is that it was started by a bunch of pilots during World War II. These guys were pretty well-off and had a high mortality rate and it became acceptable among their scene to sleep with each other's wives. The media started reporting on it in the late fifties, and even though it was considered scandalous it was pretty clear that the public was down with the trend. By the early sixties there were all sorts of magazines with ads for "swingers" and by the late sixties clubs started forming.

Swingers clubs exist all over the country and have their own sets of rules and social codes. If you want to play with other couples in a safe, casual environment then swinging might be right for you. Swinging is a primarily social activity, and swingers parties are as likely to be potlucks are they are to be orgies, so get out your recipe for Tater Tot hot-dish. You don't want to show up empty-handed.

Two types of parties exist in the swinging community: on-premise parties where people actually engage in sex on-site, and off-site parties where people engage socially and head to their own homes or hotel rooms or wherever they want to get down.

In the swinging community female bisexuality is generally accepted and encouraged; however the degree to which male bisexuality is accepted varies from scene to scene. Because of this swingers parties are mainly an option for straight couples interested in playing with another female. The swinging community also tends to be largely oriented toward vanilla sex. Those looking for a little kink will do much better at sex parties and clubs, leather events, or by hiring a professional dominant or submissive than they will at a swinging event.

The swinging scene is very accepting of different types of bodies and is populated by couples of all ages. Swingers' parties are mainly for straight couples and single bi-curious women. And they offer a perfect environment for women to explore their bi-curious desires. Dress for on-site swingers parties is usually pretty casual and people often end up running around naked at some point. You'll probably want to bring a robe or something easy to take off and put on. For off-site parties and social events people can go all out. Formal attire, fetish outfits, and all manner of fancy dress are appropriate. Sometimes the parties have themes. Generally the swinging community is very welcoming and although it might be intimidating to attend a swingers party if you've never been before, if you approach it like you would any other social activity (i.e.: be polite and friendly) you will soon find yourself feeling like a regular.

To find swingers clubs in your area check the North American Swing Club Association (NASCA listings). NASCA is an association of clubs, events, and services related to swinging and the lifestyle. If you are interested in swinging this is the place to start. An annual swingers convention, Lifestyles, is held every year and it gets rave reviews from attendees. Want to know more? Check out the resources at the end of the book.

HIRING A SEX WORKER

There are many advantages to putting your threeway in the hands of a professional. You are guaranteed a no-strings-attached, less emotionally charged experience than if you were to hook up with a friend or acquaintance. And sex workers want to make you happy. It's their job. They want your business and take pride in their work. Cruising bars can be demoralizing. When you hire a sex worker you are going to get what you set out to get.

If you have any misconceptions about sex workers being sketchy or disease-ridden you need to put them to rest. This is a bias that stems from our societal beliefs about sex being something shameful. The fact that sex work is still illegal is a huge problem, and were sex work to become legal it would make it much safer for sex workers and their clients.

GET RID OF YOUR BIASES ABOUT SEX WORKERS BY EDUCATING YOURSELF ABOUT SEX WORK. HERE IS A LIST OF BOOKS THAT MAY GIVE YOU A NEW PERSPECTIVE

- *Sex Work: Writings by Women in the Sex Industry,* Frederique Delacoste, editor
- *Women of the Light: The New Sacred Prostitute,* Kenneth Ray Stubbs, editor
- *Annie Sprinkle: Post-Porn Modernist,* Annie Sprinkle
- *Unrepentant Whore: The Collected Works of Scarlot Harlot,* Scarlot Harlot
- *Tricks and Treats: Sex Workers Write About Their Clients,* Matt Bernstein Sycamore, editor

- *Strapped for Cash: A History of American Hustler Culture*, Mack Friedman
- *Turning Pro: A Guide to Sex Work for the Ambitious and the Intrigued*, Magdalene Meretrix
- *The Male Escort's Handbook*, Aaron Lawrence

While you should always trust your instincts and not go with someone if he or she feels odd or unsafe, this is true for a stranger you'd meet in a bar as well. Most sex workers are more interested in repeat business than they are in ripping you off.

Greta Christina, author of *Paying for It: A Guide by Sex Workers for Their Customers*, suggests starting out at a strip club. "Watching your partner get a lap dance from a stripper is a good way to get an idea of how you will feel about watching your partner have sex with a sex worker."

If you are interested in a lap dance from a specific dancer, it's perfectly OK to say so. Strippers would rather you state what you want than waste their time. If someone offers you a dance and you aren't interested, a simple "No, thank you" will suffice. It's acceptable to ask them about other dancers by saying something like "Is your friend over there available?" The key is to always be polite. Sex workers are professionals and should be treated as such.

Escorts and Pro Dommes

If you are looking for something a little more intimate than a lap dance you may want to hire either an escort or a professional dominant.

Hiring an escort is a good option if what you are looking for is genital sex. Some escorts will not engage in kinky behavior so if you want an experience that includes any type of BDSM play, you should make that clear before you hire anyone. A pro domme will not engage in genital sex with you. But he or she will be perfectly willing to tie you up and spank you. And you will probably be allowed to masturbate yourself to orgasm at the end of your session, or possibly have genital sex with your partner while he or she watches.

Protocol

How you approach a sex professional depends on the type of work they are doing. You can be fairly direct with a pro domme. He or she will appreciate you stating exactly what it is you are looking for. They don't want you to leave your session unsatisfied because you never stated what it was that you wanted.

When you call up a pro domme, ask them if they work with couples. Most do and some even will take on a teaching role for couples who are interested in bringing power play and leather sex into their play. A pro domme can give you confidence, teach you to wield certain tools safely and give you confidence for when you are ready to throw your boyfriend down and play a rousing game of mistress and servant, or maybe master and slave girl if that's your bent.

According to Greta Christina when you call up a professional dominant you should have a clear idea of what you want, but do not present him or her with a script of the type of scene you want. Pro dommes take pride in their work and will run the scene creatively. "A laundry list of special requirements will make you seem pushy and will turn off a good dominant. They want to run the show."

Couples can visit a local dungeon together and hire a domme to boss them around. Or a single guy or gal can visit a dungeon solo and hire two dommes to work him or her over.

Escorts

Hiring an escort requires a slightly less direct approach. Unless you are in a Nevada brothel, prostitution is illegal. Escorts will require you to be more cagey the first time you call. "If you call up an escort and say I want you to give me a blow job and then I want you to eat my wife's pussy, he or she is going to hang up on you. Once you are an established client then you can make direct requests, but the first time will be an exercise in discretion," explains Greta Christina.

Print ads in the back of adult magazines are a good place to search for escorts. Online ads are also very good. Erosguide.com is a national directory service with listings for escorts and sex workers of all kinds. "Read an escorts ad before you call him or her. Some ads will state that they work with couples. But you should always ask." There are male escorts that will work with couples and women, but it's something that you will want to ascertain before you hire anyone. Clients of sex workers are largely single men, both gay and straight and while most escorts will be very happy to have your business they will need to know what to expect before money is exchanged. "When you hire a sex worker for your threeway, it's best if both of you are available to talk to the sex worker. If a guy calls up and says they want to hire someone to fuck his girlfriend, the sex worker might become suspicious. Both parties should discuss their desires," says Greta Christina.

Greta's Tips for Hiring a Sex Worker

1. DON'T BARGAIN. Ever. It's rude. If you can't afford someone's services, say you can't afford it and either save up some money or hire someone else.

2. A PRO DOMME will not engage in genital sex with you, but that doesn't mean they won't do other things that involve penetration of some kind. It's a good idea to ask about strap-on sex, and the like. Never push a sex worker to do something they say they don't do.

3. RESPECT YOUR SEX WORKER. Be polite.

4. BE CLEAN. Don't wear heavily scented products. Groom for your sex worker the way you would groom for a date.

5. RELAX. Sex workers are professionals. You won't be the first person who has called up and asked for a threeway.

There are many other ways to meet lovers and sex partners than I've mentioned in this chapter. But hopefully some of these suggestions will get you going. In the next chapter we will look at sex parties as places to meet new mates.

CHAPTER 4

SEX PARTIES

ANOTHER GREAT WAY TO meet your threeway players is to attend a sex party. Or maybe even throw one of your own. In this chapter we will demystify sex parties and clubs and other places people go to have public sex with multiple partners. If you aren't sure a play party is your thing, or you are very curious but a little too shy to jump right in, don't worry. This chapter will fill you in on what to expect, what to wear, how to act, and how to enjoy yourself once you are there. I'll even show you how to throw your very own sex party.

WHY ATTEND A SEX PARTY

One good way to satisfy your curiosity about multiple-partner sex, as well as maybe try on a threesome in a welcoming environment is to attend a sex party, also known as a play party. "I love going to sex parties," says the well-known performer and drag king Fudgie Frottage. "They really are a great way to hook up with a third or even start impromptu threeways. I've had it happen both ways. And sex parties are a good place to cruise since you know that the people there are there to have sex."

Play parties and sex parties are pretty much just social gatherings where people engage in sex. They take many forms and can be elaborately themed fetish parties with over a hundred people walking around in beautiful latex and leather outfits, kind of like a horny ball. Parties like these often take place in beautifully appointed dungeons that contain all sorts of fun equipment you probably don't have at home like a St. Andrews

Cross, or a sling, and can be a good way to try out new things or meet new people.

A play party can also be a regular old orgy where a bunch of enthusiastic people show up and get naked in the hot tub or a kiddie pool full of cooking oil or whatever happens to be handy. Sometimes when you get the right crowd together a regular party will become a sex party; this seems to happen a lot among the people I know. One minute everyone will be standing around gossiping and the next minute half the room has started making out.

Big or Small

My favorite sex parties are all a combination of elaborate and intimate. I love dressing up and having sex in fancy dungeons but I'm happiest when the party is on the intimate side and I know most of the people in attendance. One way to ensure your sex party experience is a good one is to decide what type of setting most appeals to you. A huge party might be overwhelming. Sometimes it's really intimidating and hard to talk to people in a really big anonymous environment. I've attended a few dungeon parties where I didn't know very many people and from time to time it just felt like too much to find new people to talk to. But on the other hand, a very large party where you don't know most of the people might offer you the anonymity you need to let go of some of your inhibitions.

The Lounge

Regardless of the type of party you attend, there will probably be a lounge area with snacks and drinks and places to lounge. If you feel uncomfortable or overwhelmed you can always head to the lounge and chat with people who aren't busy fucking. The lounge area is a great place to make some friends and find your comfort zone.

You Might Even Learn Something

Sex parties can be loads of fun. Even if you are too shy to have sex in front of lots of people, attending a sex party is a great way to join a sex-positive community and expand your network of lovers and friends. Whether or not you've had any experience with multiple-partner sex, a play party is going to introduce you to a lot of new things and help you to expand your sexual repertoire. You'll get to see new people having all different types of sex and you might learn some tricks. If you've ever been curious about flogging, play piercing, or other BDSM activities, a play party is a good place to witness these activities being performed by people who know what they are doing. And later when you become more comfortable, a play party is a great place to find willing partners and try out your new tricks. I honed my spanking skills at sex parties, first by watching skilled spanking tops dish it out and then later by spanking willing bottoms.

10 REASONS TO ATTEND A SEX PARTY

1. YOU GET TO DRESS UP in things you can't wear to the grocery store

2. YOU CAN TRY OUT equipment, like slings, that you don't have at home

3. PERFORMING for an audience can be a turn-on

4. YOU CAN CRUISE for sex partners

5. YOU CAN HAVE SEX with no strings attached

6. YOU CAN MAKE a lot of noise and no one will call the police

7. YOU'LL GET TO SEE lot of other people having sex

8. YOU CAN HAVE anonymous or group sex

9. YOU CAN MAKE new friends and join a community

10. YOU CAN LEARN new skills

WHERE TO FIND SEX PARTIES

Play parties are common in heavily populated urban areas, and asking around or checking the local papers is often all it takes to locate one. Larger parties are often held in clubs where you won't necessarily need an invite, but they may charge cover and enforce a dress code. It really depends on the town you live in and how organized the partygoing population is.

Public Clubs

There are public clubs, like bathhouses for gay men that are open twenty-fours hours a day. Other public clubs might be open all the time, but dedicate a different night of the week to a different sexual orientation; some nights are women only, some nights are dedicated to the trans community, etc.

Private Parties

Many private parties are invite-only and you may need to know someone who attends regularly in order to find out about them or to get on the invite list. As long as you are polite and open-minded there's no reason why you won't get invited—the hard part will be tracking the party down in the first place. Don't be discouraged by this; a little bit of exclusivity will make the party better and ensures that all the folks in attendance are there to play and have fun with each other, not just watch and bring the energy down.

Find One in Your Town

If you live in a small town or a very conservative city, sex parties might be harder to find. Start at the local sex shop or SM boutique and look for flyers or local papers with classified ads. Or ask the people who work there; chances are if they are working at a sex shop they are part of the sex-positive community. If you don't have any sex shops, look for an alternative newspaper or magazine at an independent bookstore; magazines often have ads in the back. If that doesn't work, head to the Internet! Get online and find a sexually oriented discussion board, or a site like craigslist.org where people often post personal ads. Post a query about sex parties in your area and see what turns up. As is usually the case with the Internet, someone will know someone who will know someone who throws sex parties.

> *I'm a man who lives in a small city in New Mexico and we don't have any organized sex events, but there are definitely kinky people here. There are lots of privately held gatherings and couples who are interested in playing with other couples or single women. We're really open to new people joining us, as long as they are sexy and into playing around.*
>
> —D, 47

LOOKING FOR SEXY STUFF IN YOUR TOWN? TRY OUT THESE WEB SITES:

- craigslist: www.craigslist.org
- Eros Guide: www.erosguide.com
- Alt.Polyamory: www.polyamory.org

SEX PARTY ETIQUETTE

You can attend a sex party solo or as a couple. In mixed-gender environments, single men often are required to follow certain rules that couples and single women aren't held to. This is mainly to encourage everyone to behave nicely. Think about it, single women aren't going to show up to sex clubs and parties if they have to worry about getting harassed by trench coat–wearing wankers, so respect the rules and everyone will have fun.

If you are an orgy-virgin, the best way to have fun at a sex party is to lower your expectations and realize that real life isn't like *La Dolce Vita* or *Caligula*. Fudgie Frottage advises, "I always tell myself I'm going out to have fun, not necessarily to get laid. It's not good to have really high expectations about the evening because it's too easy to get disappointed. But for the most part I'd say if someone is interested in having sex at a sex party, there's no real reason why they shouldn't be able to. I've always found someone to have sex with when I've wanted it. Though there have been times when there was no one at a party that I was attracted to."

Be Polite

A sex party is going to be full of regular people, some of whom you will find attractive and some of whom you won't. You should always be polite, have firm boundaries, keep an open mind, and be nice to people who approach you even if you don't want to have sex with them. No one likes a jerk.

Don't stand around chatting loudly when people nearby are busy fucking. You might think the story about taking your nephew to the zoo is totally hilarious but the lovely girl in the sling next to you might be distracted by your voice. You wouldn't want a stranger ruining your orgasm, would you? Well neither does she.

Mixed Parties

If you are attending a mixed-gender shindig, oftentimes referred to as a pansexual, or omnisexual party, then all sorts of differently gendered and bodied people will be playing with each other. It's not uncommon, especially in the BDSM scene, for people to play with a gender that they wouldn't usually have regular old sex with. For instance, a woman might be interested in flogging and caning another woman but not want to engage in vanilla sex with her. Or a butch daddy top might get her boots worshipped by a bio boy but not necessarily want to fuck him.

One butch-femme dyke couple I know regularly attend mixed gender sex parties and engage in scenes with straight men, usually as part of some kind of power play. For instance if they are involved in daddy/girl roleplay, daddy will make his little girl suck off a line of strange men. They both get off on these types of scenes but would never play with bio males outside of a play party atmosphere.

Another lesbian couple I know attend play parties separately. One of them is bisexual and enjoys playing with men. Her girlfriend is comfortable with her bisexuality and public playing, but isn't necessarily into watching her partner with guys. So they go solo. Miss bi girl goes to play parties where she can have fun with boys without worrying that her girlfriend will be uncomfortable. If you are attending a pansexual party there's no rule stating that you have to have sex with a gender you aren't comfortable with, but you should understand that everyone is there to have fun and keep your judgments to yourself.

You and Your Partner

If you are attending as a couple, talk about your relationship before you get there. All sorts of situations will come up and you don't want to find yourself having a disagreement in public. Set rules with your partner beforehand and stick to them in public.

Dress for Sexcess

It's important to dress for a sex party. But what you wear is going to depend on what type of party it is. Some parties will ask you to check your clothes at the door, some will require the guests to dress in sexy underwear. If the party has no particular theme it's OK to wear something very revealing that you feel comfortable and sexy in. Nothing says hot and ready-to-fuck like a gay man or a hot butch dyke in ripped Levis. And a gorgeous woman in a corset is going to be welcome anywhere. Other suggestions include lingerie, jock straps, leather pants, PVC, skimpy dresses, stripper wear, porn star outfits, boxer shorts, cross dressing attire, or vintage girdles and slips. If you find yourself attending play parties regularly you'll probably want to invest in a few items of clothing to wear. They don't have to be expensive, but you'll want access to clothes and things that make you feel sexy.

Themes

If the party has a theme, then by all means follow it. If it's a leather or uniform party don't wear Bermuda shorts or you'll look silly. Dressing the part will help you fit in and feel comfortable. And if you are new to a particular party scene, it's a sign of respect to dress the part. It shows you care.

One night after a lovely dinner in the Castro, San Francisco's sexy, queer district, my best gal pal and I headed into a nearby bar for a beer. The bartender politely informed us that particular bar was having an underwear party that night and while we were welcome to stay we should be respectful to all the guys in their skivvies. We checked out the back room; it was full of gay men engaging in public sex. While we weren't necessarily into getting busy (or welcome to join in for that matter), we figured what the hell and took off our skirts and sat in our panties while we drank our beer. The gesture was much appreciated by the patrons, and many party attendees told us they enjoyed having us sitting around in our Victoria's Secret undies while a hundred gay men were sucking each other off in the next room. So, dress up and fit in, because it's really all about being a good sport.

Bring a Friend

If you are feeling nervous about attending your first sex party alone, bring a friend along. But make sure it's a friend you feel comfortable having sex in front of; you never know when you might find yourself bent over a saw horse with your knickers around your ankles.

When to Arrive

Plan your arrival time so that you won't be the first person there standing around by yourself. You also don't want to get there so late that everyone has already separated into little piles of humping bodies. Arriving somewhere in the middle will ensure you have time to cruise.

Meeting People

Relax, be friendly, have fun. If you are there as a couple to pick up a third, don't act too aggressively. Scope the room for singles and approach them in a sexy, nonthreatening way. Compliment the person, ask politely if they would like to play with you and your partner. If you are a straight couple looking for a threeway it's important for both of you to negotiate with any potential dates. Nothing says creepy power-imbalance like a couple where the guy does all the talking. The room may very well be crawling with single ladies who want to fuck a couple, but they are going to be turned off in a situation where it seems like the wife isn't as interested as the husband. Many a threeway has been ruined by an overeager participant. "I got approached by a cute guy at a party and he asked me if I liked to play with girls and if I'd be interested in playing with his girlfriend. I said yes but I wished she had asked me instead of him because it made it seem like she wasn't as into the idea," says sex columnist Jamye Waxman.

Fudgie Frottage says "I was at a San Francisco sex party on New Year's Eve. It had a red light district theme and you got the fake dollars to hand out to people to buy their favors. My date got handed a fake twenty by some dude who wanted her to make out with his wife. They were really having a good time. It seemed like everyone was making out with his wife. I'm pretty sure he was looking to find a threeway but he was still trying when we left."

Don't Stare

Don't stare at people who are getting it on. Of course being a horny voyeur is part of the game, but staring mouth agape will make you seem like a freak. Don't get too close to people's scenes unless you are invited in and never ever touch anyone without permission. If you are at a dungeon party, lounging around on the equipment is bad manners unless, of course, you are lounging naked waiting for someone to come jump you.

Don't push people to do things they aren't into. A person might agree to make out with you but not want to go any further; that's within their right and aggressively pursuing sex with someone who doesn't want to have it is going to keep you from getting invited back.

Regardless of your gender or what type of party you happen to be at, if you flirt, make eye contact, chat people up, and act confident, you'll get more attention than you'll know what to do with.

Follow Rules

Most play spaces will have a list of rules posted in plain sight. Follow them. They will probably state the level of safe-sex precautions you are required to follow and the space will most likely provide safer-sex supplies. It is downright rude to engage in unsafe sex at a sex party where safer sex is required, even if you and your partner are fluid-bonded, meaning you've been tested for everything and have agreed to play only with each other.

Dealing with Pushy People

If you are having sex at the party and someone intrudes on your space, it's perfectly acceptable to tell them to leave. Be firm, let the person know they aren't welcome. If they refuse to leave, make the host aware of the situation. If you are at a large public place, there will most likely be dungeon monitors; find one and tell them about the problem.

Top Ten Sex Party Faux Pas

1. WEARING street clothes to a fetish party
2. CROWDING a scene
3. STARING or being judgmental
4. TOUCHING someone without permission
5. MAKING comments about people, bodies, or appearances
6. NEGLECTING to clean up after yourself
7. KISSING and telling
8. BORROWING someone's toys without permission
9. HAVING unsafe sex
10. SHOWING UP drunk

CRUISING

Sometimes just having sex with your date at a sex party will end up feeling like a threeway. You can pretty much expect to have an audience and, depending on what type of party you are at, you could become the entertainment. Keep in mind a sex party is public, meaning you aren't necessarily going to meet your ideal third person and run home to have sex in private, though that can happen. Be open to anything and your evening will be much more fun. If you are going to a sex party with the goal of picking up someone there are a few rules to follow to make it easier.

> *I'm a woman who likes like going to play parties and watching other people's scenes. I've never picked up anyone at a party, but I've had sex with lovers at play parties. Usually we get a small audience and there's been a few times where I've handed a paddle off to someone and let them spank my girlfriend. I'd say overall my play party experiences have been really positive. And I could definitely see going to a play party if I was specifically looking for someone to watch me have sex.*
>
> —K, 42

Cruising at sex parties is like cruising anywhere else, but at least you can be sure that the people present are there to get laid. Good cruising is sexy without being intrusive. It's perfectly acceptable to make the guests feel admired, but walking up to them and wanking off on their legs is bad manners. Don't laugh! It happens. The last time I went to a certain local San Francisco sex club some guy in a trench coat followed me around all night yanking feverishly on his flaccid penis. I haven't gone back to that club since.

Make eye contact. A slow gaze that lasts a beat longer than it should, followed by a smile is a widely recognized and very seductive come on. But a really obvious leer makes you look desperate. Flattery will get you everywhere. If you find someone attractive, tell them.

Make friends with people at the party. Friends are great allies and can help by introducing you to someone you might like. If you do see someone you like, introduce yourself. "Hi, my name is Diana," is a better start than "Wanna fuck?" Though, sometimes that approach works, too.

It's normal for sex-party attendees to chat a bit and then be pretty direct about wanting to play. If you want to play with someone, ask directly. It's as simple as saying "Would you like to play with me?" If they say no, be polite. If they say yes, you'll want to negotiate your boundaries and fantasies about what follows. Be very clear about what you are looking for. And if you want to engage in any kind of SM play, make that known. Negotiating means talking about what types of things you want and are willing to do. It doesn't mean persuading someone to have certain types of sex with you.

Be clear about your limits, talk openly about your fantasies and expectations, and don't ever feel like you need to apologize for your desire.

> *The last time I went to a local women's BDSM party I saw a threeway I will never forget. There was a young femme up on a table on all fours, and she was wearing a butt plug and a collar and was getting fisted really hard by an older butch woman. Another femme in heels and PVC seemed to be directing the action. The collared femme was begging the woman who was fucking her to let her come. Really begging loudly, nearly screaming. And the femme in the PVC outfit kept saying "No, she doesn't get to come yet." It was the hottest thing I'd ever seen in my life.*
>
> —E, 37

JOINING A SCENE IN PROGRESS

Let's say you happen to be witness to a scene so hot it sets your pants on fire. And you can't help but want to join in on the action.

Well, it's possible that the participants will welcome you if you approach them correctly.

Begin by closing the distance between you and the players. Be aware of your body language; crossed arms makes you seem angry or closed off. Try and look as relaxed and open as you can muster. Don't crowd the folks playing, but get close enough to make eye contact.

Wait for one of the scene participants to recognize your desire and smile at them. If they acknowledge your smile you can come a little closer. If this doesn't spur a rejection, then it's ok to ask "May I join you?" And if you are welcomed in, congratulations! Just join in on the action in a nonintrusive way. Get busy, and save the introductions for after. No one gives a shit what your name is while they have a dick in their mouth. Wait till the post-orgasm afterglow for chitchat.

THROW YOUR OWN SEX PARTY

Tired of Scrabble? Bored with Boggle? Can't bring yourself to attend another *L Word* party? Why not invite your friends over for sex? If what you're really looking for is group sex—threeways, exhibitionism and voyeurism, with maybe a little light BDSM on the side—a sex soiree is really the way to go. As truly great sex parties can be hard to find outside of big cities with adventurous populations, throwing your own is a good way to ensure it ends up being a serious throw down.

Throwing a sex party isn't really all that different from throwing a regular party. You'll want to invite people who you think will click, set up a space for people to party, guest-proof a few things, maybe set a dress code, decorate a bit, pick out music and videos to inspire everyone, and make some delicious snacks.

The Guest List

Your guest list is the most important part of the planning. You know your friends, and you probably have some idea of which friends will click. Ideally you'll invite a decent balance of genders and orientations, tops and bottoms, that type of thing. You don't want to end up with a room full of leather daddies all scoping each other and no one to get down on all fours, and conversely a room full of bottoms saying "You do me first," "No, you do me first," isn't going to work either.

It's difficult to predict how everyone will act in a group setting, so just do your best. When deciding how many people you can comfortably accommodate, make sure to picture them all prone while you are doing the math. Fifty people standing around sipping sidecars takes up less space than fifty people reenacting the Kama Sutra.

Create a basic guest list and augment it with sexy strangers. Make yourself some flyers and carry them with you. Anytime you see a potential attendee hand them an invite.

The Play Space

You can throw a sex party anywhere—basements, empty warehouses, suites at the W—it really doesn't matter. But for the purpose of this article let's assume you'll be throwing it in your own humble abode. You'll want to create a lot of horizontal space. Clear most of the furniture out of whatever rooms you'll be using. Couches can stay, and so can ottomans, but coffee tables and such just take up room. A series of large cushions on the floor, and lots of blankets to protect the guests from rug burn will work very well. Include a few padded mats, an air mattress if you have one, and any other comfy inviting props you can think of. Dim the lights and turn the heat up. Think love den, like Greg Brady's room in the *Brady Bunch* episode where he moved to the attic.

Keep Their Hands and Mouths Busy

Sexy snacks are an important ingredient. Sex makes people

hungry and you'll want a place for folks to gather and take a break from the action or cruise their next playmate. The kitchen is the obvious place to serve treats, but a lounge area, like maybe a bedroom will work as well.

Stick with easy to handle finger foods, nothing too heavy or sticky, and preferably things that don't take too much preparation. Sandwiches are good, so are bowls of nuts and dried fruit. A cheese plate, a few baguettes, some crudités, chips, and pretzels are also good options. Lay out some some cookies and chocolate for the sweet-toothed among you. You can certainly go fancier if you prefer, and a nice spread will encourage lots of eating and socializing. But a table filled with delicious basics will keep folks satisfied. It's fine to serve libations, sipping wine can help get everyone in the mood. But avoid having a full bar; no one wants to have sex with a room full of drunk folks. It's not safe or sexy.

Get the Party Started

Assign tasks to a few select helpers. The person answering the door should introduce everyone. Offer your guests a place to check their clothes. If some fancy dressers prefer to keep their latex catsuits on, ask them to at least check their shoes; seven inch stilettos are dangerous around dangly naked parts. Assign a few other friends the task of making out at various stages of the evening. Sometimes the guests need permission to get busy. Having a few enthusiastic sex hounds seed the party will go a long way toward making everyone comfortable and getting the action started.

Keep Your Supplies Handy

As the host it's your responsibility to provide all the safer sex supplies. Chances are people will pack their own toys, lube and latex, but you should stock the room very well and be prepared for anything. Several bottles of lube of various consistencies should be within reach. Put dental dams, latex gloves, and condoms in bowls all around the room. You'll also want to provide sharps containers for piercing scenes, and lots of receptacles for used latex. Other necessities include towels, baby wipes, a First Aid kit, absorbent pads for serious squirters, and a clean place for people to wash up.

Set the Scene

Entertainment is key. You might want to schedule some performances—maybe even instructional ones. Think of this trick as a way of prepping the guests to have fun just like the free lessons you get before you go salsa dancing. Have some folks agree to put on a little sexy workshop to inspire everyone and bolster their confidence. And regardless of whether you have live sex shows, you want some porn videos playing in the background to inspire people and give them something to look at while they are resting.

Pick the videos carefully. Find stuff that will actually inspire people and not turn them off; avoid triggering subject matter like race fetish and rape scenes. Indie dyke porn is always popular, unless you're in a room full of gay men I suppose. If your party is mixed in terms of gender and sexual orientation, then pick out a variety.

Aural Pleasure

If you can get someone to DJ your party, great! But if not, a few well-planned mix CDs will work just fine. Everyone's idea of sexy music is different but soft ambient stuff is safe. You'll want to pick songs that flow into each other and create a mood. Keep it mellow, nothing jarring. Recently I was having sex with my iTunes on shuffle in the background. Unfortunately, and also embarrassingly, "The Toreador Song" from Bizet's *Carmen* came on very loudly at a pivotal moment. Don't let this happen to you.

Create play lists and use them judiciously. Music with really recognizable lyrics can be distracting when you are having sex. As much as you might love to rock out to Tori Amos you probably don't want the girl below you to start belting out tunes while you are fucking her.

•••

Now that you know what to expect at a sex party and even how to throw your own little sex shindig, it's time for some advanced sex lessons. In the next chapter you'll learn some anatomy lessons they probably didn't cover in school. Pay close attention because knowing the lay of the land is the best way to become a great lover.

CHAPTER 5

ANATOMY LESSONS FOR LOVERS

UNDERSTANDING YOUR BODY AND the body of your lovers is one of the most important aspects of a great sex life. While it's true that there's a lot more involved in truly great sex than just the parts behind your zipper, men and women of all orientations, genders, and bodies could be having a lot more fun if they were well informed about what's going on down there. And part of the purpose of this book is to get you to play with a body type that you might not be all that experienced with. Besides, knowing the names of all the good parts will come in handy if you find yourself on *Jeopardy!* So study up on the body basics and know before you go.

> *My first threeway was with two girls. I think of myself as a lesbian now, but back then I was bisexual for all intents and purposes. I had been really flirty with two of my friends. Three of us got naked and crawled into my California King. It was probably one of my favorite sexual experiences mainly because none of us had any roles or preconceived notions about what we wanted to do. It was just three naked girls all playing with each other. I'm not actually sure anyone really got off, it wasn't particularly goal-oriented. But it sure as hell was great.*
>
> —S, 32

None of us are born sack artists. We learn to be good at sex by paying attention to the responses we get when we try something new. We improve our skills when we pay attention to the physical and visual clues that our lovers give us. We also learn by communicating, asking questions, and paying attention to our own bodies and what feels good. Our sexual response evolves over time. The things that turned you on when you were a teenager probably look nothing like the things that you get off on as an adult. Otherwise we'd all be getting off thinking about unicorns and Sears catalog underwear models.

> *I've always wanted to suck a cock. I've had threeways with two guys and a girl before, but the guys didn't really seem into the idea of touching anything that wasn't a female body part. I don't know if I'd be any good at it, but I figure it's a cock and it's not that complicated. And I have one of my own so I could probably figure it out.*
>
> —A, 28

•••

> *I've had sex with lots of guys with boyfriends. I actually prefer sex with couples because it keeps it from getting too serious.*
>
> —K, 26

When we are just starting out sexually we don't really understand the full potential of a fabulous sex life. Let's be honest here, usually as sexual newcomers (bad pun intended) we're too excited by the prospect of actually having sex to get critical about it. It's really only after we've had years of experience that we start to figure out just how much potential there is to have freaky fun in bed. This isn't to say that simple make-out sessions with new lovers aren't exciting. But there's always room to take things to another level and that's really what this book is about.

Same-sex couples have an advantage in the anatomy-knowledge department because they have at least some idea of the basics and their functions, though it's a bad idea to assume that everyone else's parts work the same way yours do. If you're sexually driven enough to want a threeway you probably understand that no two bodies are exactly alike.

> *I love having my pussy licked, but my butch girlfriend would laugh at me if I tried to do that to her.*
>
> —K, 24

Couples with different bodies and genders have even more to learn about each other, and while it's good for all of us to learn to talk to each other about our needs and desires, we can't always count on our lovers to tell us everything there is to know. He or she might not entirely understand his or her own body and sexual response, and even if he or she does there are other factors to consider. Perhaps your special friend is embarrassed to talk to you about what she likes and how she wants to be touched. Or maybe he just hasn't figured it all out yet. But with a good strong understanding of everything going on below the belt, you'll have an idea about what questions to ask. Now, with that said, when you have two lovers in your bed, well that's all the more terrain to cover.

LEARNING THE LAY OF THE LAND

If you've always wanted to get up close and personal with a pussy, but you've never touched one that isn't attached to you, or you're curious about cocks but too shy to get past second base, this basic schooling should help you out.

I've had relationships with both men and women, but I've never gotten to have both at the same time. Every time I get close one of the parties chickens out. I'm a bi girl, but I've never dated another woman who identifies as bi, all my girlfriends have been lesbians. I'd like to be in a relationship where anything goes, but I just haven't found it yet.

—K, 28

Before we get into all the different things three people can do in a bed, I'd like to take you on a guided tour of human sexual anatomy. You can make this chapter fun by dropping your pants, grabbing a big hand mirror and following along. No matter what you've got going on between your legs it's a good idea to get to know it. And while you're down there you can experiment with some new maneuvers, teach yourself a few tricks to try out on your lovers later.

On the surface girl parts and boy parts don't seem to have much in common. But the truth is they really aren't that different. Both sets of genitals are formed from the same embryonic nub (to use a technical term) and it's only a hormone bath that tells the tissue whether to become a pussy or a dick. In other words, every part of the vulva has a corresponding penis part.

SO, YOU HAVE A PENIS?

There are no bones in your boner, and there aren't any muscles either, at least not in the shaft. The shaft of your basic run-of-the-mill penis is made up of three columns of spongy erectile tissue and blood vessels that run down the length. Two of these columns run along the top of your dick and are called the *corpus cavernosa*. One runs along the bottom of your dick and surrounds the urethra. This one is called the *corpus spongeosum*. The corpus spongeosum is connected to the head of the penis, called the *glans*. When you get turned on these babies all fill with blood, and *schwing!* That's the magic ingredient to a hard-on.

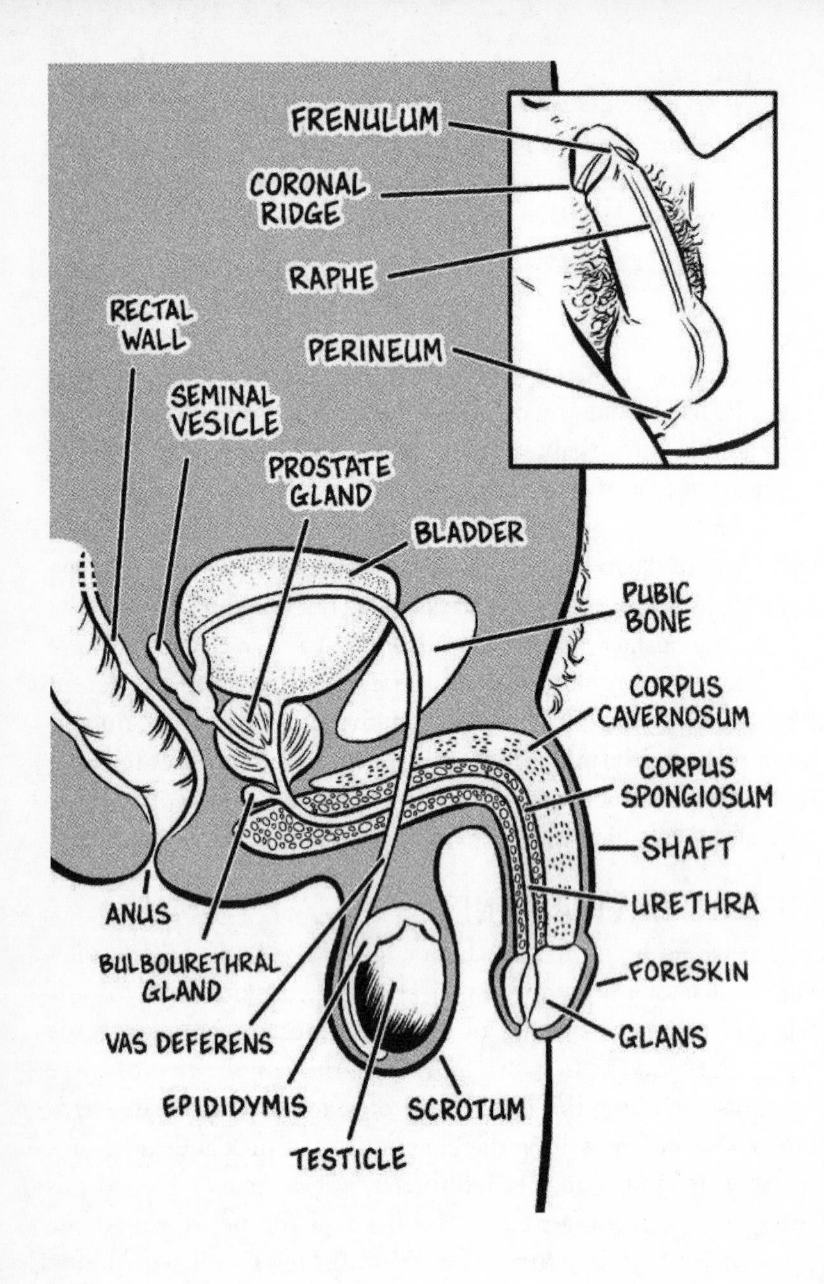
FRENULUM
CORONAL RIDGE
RAPHE
RECTAL WALL
PERINEUM
SEMINAL VESICLE
PROSTATE GLAND
BLADDER
PUBIC BONE
CORPUS CAVERNOSUM
CORPUS SPONGIOSUM
SHAFT
URETHRA
ANUS
BULBOURETHRAL GLAND
FORESKIN
GLANS
VAS DEFERENS
EPIDIDYMIS
SCROTUM
TESTICLE

I really get off on watching guys have sex. I've had a lot of threeways, but half the time I just watch and jerk off.

—K, 41

The base of the penis extends all the way back into the body, practically back to your butthole. So, in other words, some of your shaft is actually internal. The internal portion of the penis is called the *root*, or the *bulb*. You've probably heard of penis lengthening surgery, which involves cutting of two ligaments that support some of the penis shaft internally. Release of these ligaments allows more of the shaft to protrude from the body.

You do not want this. Not at all. Your penis is perfectly wonderful, trust me on this. Under no circumstances should you consider getting a Frankenpenis. I like your penis the way it is and so does your boyfriend or girlfriend.

The first part of the penis to greet you on your guided penis tour is the head, also called the *glans*. The head has the highest concentration of nerve endings in the whole package, though considerably less than a clit, sorry boys! Look at the center of the head of your penis, or whoever's penis you happen to be following along with and you will see the urethral opening, often unglamorously referred to as the piss slit because of course it's what you pee through. Though the head of the penis is the most nerve-rich section, men sometimes complain that the head is desensitized after circumcision. Possibly because circumcision leaves the glans exposed to constant contact and the poor thing becomes overloaded and desensitized as a defense maneuver. There is a movement against circumcision for this very reason.

Your next stop on the penis tour is the coronal ridge or the crown. This is the raised ridge around the head, and it is what gives the head its mushroom shape. Look underneath the ridge and find the spot where the head connects to the shaft. This spot is called the *frenulum*. This is a sweet, sensitive spot for a tongue to linger or a place to pay some extra attention to during a hand job. While you are looking at the underneath part of your or your boyfriend's dick, note that raised section along the bottom, running from the coronal ridge down the shaft and over the middle of the testicles to the anus. That's called the *raphe*.

> *I think the most sensitive part of my penis is its pride*
>
> —I, 34

Many men find that in addition to the frenulum the raphe is also an extra-sensitive area of the shaft. The internal portion of the penis ends behind the balls and can be felt by pressing the *perineum*, the area between the testicles and anus. One of the reasons it feels good to get fucked in the ass is that it stimulates the root of the penis through the rectal wall.

The foreskin is the baggy layer of skin that covers the head on uncircumcised cocks; it's what makes a cock look like a snake wearing a turtleneck. An estimated two thirds of American men are circumcised at birth, meaning they have no foreskin, though thankfully the trend is moving away from the automatic snip snip. The head of an uncircumcised cock is nicely protected and therefore, extra sensitive. Keep this in mind and use it to your advantage!

One more little thing about the foreskin: it functions as a fun moveable sheath over the dick so you can give yourself, your boyfriend, or your neighbor a lube-free handjob. But if you are cut, don't sweat it! That's what lube is for, right?

> *It's perfectly normal for your dick to curve up, down, or sideways. Just like pussies, no two are exactly alike.*

Right behind your dick, hanging there in a fleshy sac called the *scrotum*, are your testicles, or, er, your balls. Testicles vary in size and are temperature sensitive; they need to be a few degrees cooler than body temperature in order to produce sperm, their *job*. In order to keep cool the balls move up and down in the scrotum in a sort of self-regulating AC system. And yes, this is the reason for shrinkage. When you get out of that freezing cold pool your balls pull up against your nice warm body for safety.

Balls are very sensitive to pain, although a lot of guys get into CBT or cock and ball torture. You can buy all sorts of fun things for your balls including ball stretchers, cock cages, and weights and clamps to attach to your scrotum.

The vas deferens are two small tubes that connect the epididymis (a sort of storage facility for sperm) to the urethra. The vas deferens get cut during a vasectomy. The seminal vesicles sort of sound like something from catechism school, but really they are just glands that produce nutrients for semen.

The bulbourethral glands secrete a clear fluid known as pre-cum, or pre-ejaculate if you want to get technical. They are located behind the urethra.

Semen, or cum, or maybe come, depending on what dictionary you are using, is the fluid that squirts out when you ejaculate. The testicles make the sperm and when you get turned on the sperm move out of the testes into the epididymis, then through the vas deferens, and then into the urethra where they mix it up with a couple of bodily fluids to produce semen. This mixture is expelled through your urethra when you ejaculate.

The prostate gland produces some of the fluid that helps transport sperm. It's located behind the public bone, below the bladder, and is analogous to the female G spot. It feels good when you prod and poke it, one of the many reasons that boys enjoy getting banged in the butt.

The best time I ever had with two guys was this night my friend and I hooked up with this other guy who was a total slutty bottom. We both fucked him in the ass simultaneously. It was a little difficult, but we made it work. He loved it.

—S, 27

Hard-ons

Sometimes dicks just get hard. This is the autonomic nervous system taking over. For instance, men get boners in their sleep. Teenage boys get them randomly, often in the most embarrassing situations. However, it's really the on-purpose boners we're talking about here. The muscles that control the blood supply to the penis are normally tense and keep the blood flow at bay; however when you get excited they relax and allow blood to flow into your dick, and *bingo!* you get hard. As the dick fills with blood, the surrounding membrane becomes taught, like an inflated balloon. This squeezes the veins that would normally allow the blood to flow back out of the penis creating, you guessed it, a raging hard-on.

An erect dick can hold eight times as much blood as a flaccid one. But cocks do not expand in any kind of direct correlation to their nonerect size.

In other words, you can be a shower not a grower but pretty much once it gets hard it's about the same size as everyone else's.

Average size of a flaccid penis: 3.5 inches
Average size of an erect penis: 5.1 – 5.8 inches

All sorts of drugs can affect your erection. Some substances, like cocaine, can prevent you from having an orgasm. And other substances, like alcohol, can prevent you from getting hard in the first place. Viagra works by causing the relaxation of the muscles and vesicles, thereby allowing your dick to fill up with blood. Poppers do the same thing. Cock rings can keep blood in the penis, making an erection last longer.

WHAT LADIES HAVE

The lady parts you can see externally are generally referred to as the *vulva*. The vulva includes everything you can see between a pair of parted legs. And if you are looking at one right now, then lucky you.

The *mons* is the first thing you see between a pair of naked thighs. It's covered in pubic hair, unless you remove it.

The next thing you see if you spread your legs is the outer labia, or *labia majora*. These are also covered in hair on the outside, but the inside is smooth and covered in oil glands. Like most parts of a pussy, the outer labes are very sensitive to touch. They are analogous to the scrotum in men and are very fleshy and padded. They are designed to cover up all the sensitive parts inside, though in some ladies the inner lips and clitoral hood extend past the outer lips. This is one of these times where I feel it necessary to remind you that all genitals look different. So if yours don't look like the ones you see in *Playboy*, don't fret. They touch those up in Photoshop, you know.

Next we have the inner labia, or *labia minora*. These are the slippery little lips on the inside. They can be very small and tidy or long and unruly and most of the time they don't match up; one is often longer or wider or darker than the other. They look different on every lady. The inner lips are more sensitive than the outer lips and many women enjoy having them licked and fondled. These lips surround the head of the clit or *glans*, the urethral opening, and the opening to your vagina—known as the *introitus*, but please don't ever call it that during sex.

The head of the clit is covered in folds of tissue called the *hood*. The hood protects the sensitive glans of the clit. If you pull back the skin you'll see the glans in all its pink glory and that's the part we're usually talking about when we say clit.

People used to think that's all there was to the clitoris, but in recent years we've gotten a little smarter about female anatomy

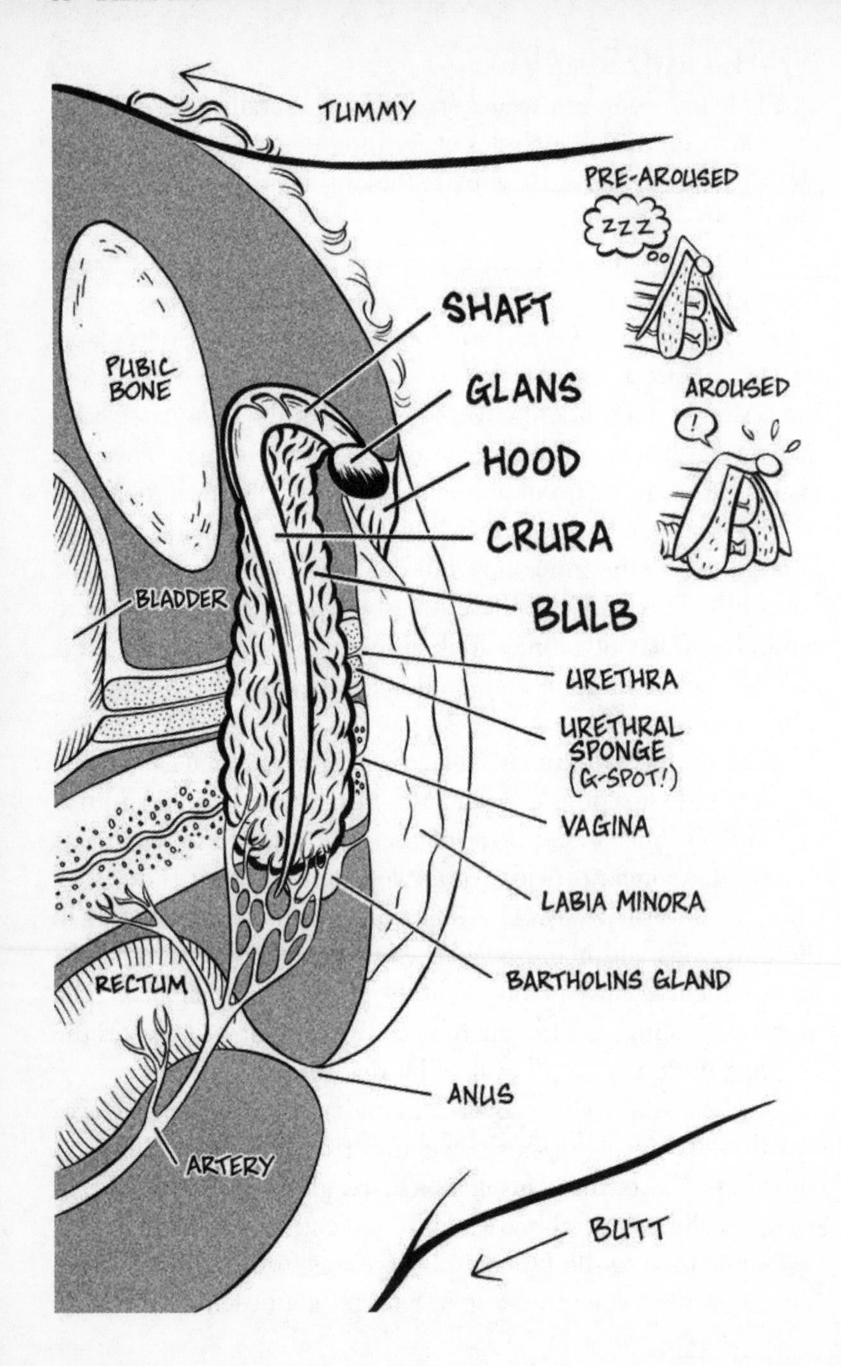
TUMMY
PRE-AROUSED
ZZZ
SHAFT
GLANS
HOOD
CRURA
BULB
AROUSED
!
PUBIC BONE
BLADDER
URETHRA
URETHRAL SPONGE (G-SPOT!)
VAGINA
LABIA MINORA
BARTHOLINS GLAND
RECTUM
ANUS
ARTERY
BUTT

and female sexual response. Finally we get it, and we've gotten over all that silly crap about vaginal orgasms and clitoral ones. Anytime you dial O on the pink telephone it's due to stimulation of the clit, be it internal or external.

The clit has eighteen different parts. That's a lot of parts, but don't worry I won't quiz you. Just keep in mind that it's a complex organ that pretty much extends throughout your entire genital region. The glans is crazy with nerve endings. In fact, there are about eight thousand of them. This thing is sensitive, so be very careful with it. Just like cocks, clits vary greatly in size. But size really doesn't correlate to sensitivity; so don't worry about it if you have a small one. When a woman is aroused, the clit fills up with blood and gets hard, just like a cock. It expands in size and peeks out from its protective hood and looks like a mini hard-on.

If you feel around under the hood you'll find a rubbery cord extending up from the glans. This is the clitoral shaft. The shaft connects to the glans and the legs of the clit, also known as the *clitoral crura*. The clitoral crura are internal and extend back from the shaft in a sort of wishbone shape. These legs are partly responsible for making vaginal penetration so delicious. There aren't a great deal of nerve endings on the vaginal walls, otherwise childbirth would be a hell of a lot more difficult than it already is. But the internal parts of the clitoris respond to pressure and friction. This is why some of us have orgasms from penetration without direct stimulation of the head of the clitoris. For the most part, however, it takes direct clitoral stimulation to bring a woman to orgasm.

What About the G spot?

The G spot, or urethral sponge is a spongy gland that surrounds the urethra. It's not really a magical spot; it's just a sensitive region of the genitals where a great deal of nerves are located and crisscrossing all over each other. You can find it by sticking two fingers in your special lady friend's vagina and curving them up toward the top, as if you were going to rub the clit from the back. The ridgy, bumpy area is the G spot. If she's new to this kind of stimulation she might not know what to make of it. For some people it's fantastic, for others it just feels like you have to pee. The G spot responds quite nicely to pressure, and once you get used to the sensations it's possible to orgasm this way. During arousal the sponge fills up with fluid and if you press on it while she's coming, it's quite possible that your special lady friend will squirt all over the place.

Squirty Girls

If you are an ejaculator, great! If not, don't worry about it. It's lots of fun, but it doesn't have a lot of bearing on the strength of your Os.

You can teach yourself to ejaculate if that's something you are interested in doing. There are many great books on the topic and lots of videos and information on the Web. Try bearing down rather than pulling in as you reach orgasm. This in itself might cause a gusher. Usually though, ejaculating requires some sort of pressure on the urethral gland during your climax. Fingers work very well, so do curved sex toys. Anything firm enough to apply a lot of pressure, but small enough in diameter so that it doesn't block the urethra is a good bet to make someone squirt.

For the longest time I was always the ejaculating half of the couple, and while my lovers seemed to enjoy the show I was neither here nor there about it. It didn't necessarily make my orgasms stronger, and while I enjoyed the whole process I didn't feel it was a necessary component of a great fuck. Then I met a gal who ejaculated when she got off and suddenly I understood why my former lovers had gone so crazy over it. Getting a woman off like that and being drenched in her fluids afterward is just about the biggest thrill ride out there. Forget the Sparkletts Water Fantasy at SeaWorld; it's more like Space Mountain meets the Drop Zone at Great America.

THE GENDER-FREE PARTS

Both guys and gals have a series of pelvic muscles called the *Pubococcygeal muscles*, better known as the PC muscles. These are the muscles that spasm when you come. If you strengthen them you can increase the strength and duration of your orgasms, and who doesn't want that?

HOW TO EXERCISE YOUR PC MUSCLES:

1. THINK ABOUT PEEING. If you are really unfamiliar with this territory, you might want to actually pee during this exercise. Now, squeeze the muscles you would use to cut off the stream of pee. Got it? The muscles you use to do this are your PC muscles. Now you've found them.

2. SQUEEZE AND RELEASE YOUR MUSCLES AS MANY TIMES AS YOU CAN FOR ONE MINUTE. Try varying the rhythm to keep it exciting. Then squeeze and hold the tension for as long as you can. If you are female-bodied, strengthening these muscles will help you to enjoy sex more, have stronger orgasms, and will prevent bladder problems later in life. If you are male-bodied, strengthening this muscle can help you develop control over your ejaculations.

3. SQUEEZE YOUR BUTTHOLE. No, seriously. Do it. It is also part of the PC loop. Follow the instructions above, only squeezing and releasing your anus this time. We all carry a lot of tension down there, and you don't want to be a tight-ass, do you? Relaxing and strengthening this muscle will make all types of sex more enjoyable and it's absolutely necessary if you want to enjoy anal sex.

Let's Hear It for the Butt

Everyone has a butthole. Face it, the butthole is an equal opportunity orifice. It's just a hole. It's not weird, bad, or wrong to want to stick things up your butt or someone else's. Anal sex is fun. Your butthole has tons of blood vessels and nerve endings; in other words it is very sensitive. And in the context of a threeway, the more holes the better.

The opening to your ass is called the *anus*. The area around your anus is full of hair follicles, this means everyone has hair down there. So get over your worries about it. If you are totally hairless between your cheeks it's either because you remove the hair, you are a pre-teen, or you are a freak of nature. If you are really hairy and you feel self-conscious about it, you can get it waxed. Lots of salons offer something called a "tweeny wax" which pretty much consists of waxing between your butt cheeks.

The anal opening is controlled by two bands of muscle called the *sphincters*. The external sphincter muscle is closest to the opening and if you pay lots of attention to your Kegels, you can learn to relax and contract this baby at will. The inner sphincter muscle is controlled by your autonomic nervous system (the autonomic nervous system controls all involuntary bodily functions like breathing and heart rate). The internal sphincter muscle reacts involuntarily, i.e., it relaxes and allows feces to move when you are ready to go.

The stretch of skin starting right below the vulva in women, and below the testes in men is called the *perineum*. It's basically the no-mans-land between your cooch or your balls and your butthole. It's full of nerve endings and stroking it can feel amazing. Pay lots of attention to this little area, it's very sensitive.

Your rectum is the tube that transports waste from the large intestine to the anus. It's not technically a sexual organ but many people into advanced anal play, i.e., fisting and or very large toys, report states of extreme euphoria after a session of intense anal play.

YOUR ANATOMY IS NOT YOUR DESTINY

> *I like when my girlfriend wears my clothes. She looks like a little boy.*
>
> —D, 30

Straight or queer, we've all had experience with our culture's rigid gender categories. The rules say that each biological sex has its own gender, and no mixing it up is allowed. The idea that gender is binary with female on one end and male on the other is silly and restrictive. There are all sorts of rules about appropriate "masculine" behavior and "feminine" behavior: ways of dressing, speaking, acting, even career choices are all seen as dictated by what's between our legs.

Gender is a social construct completely separate from what you happen to be packing beneath your 501s, and while this idea is something that many queers have embraced, any straight girl who pines after fey, long-haired, indie-rock boys has at least some idea of what I'm talking about.

Sometimes It's Just an Outfit

For some of us, gender is just a fun toy to play with. For instance, I'm a high femme lesbian. I'm talking really high femme and really high heels. But my friends routinely refer to me as a frat boy in a skirt. What they see as my horny, sexually predatory personality doesn't gel with how they picture a very feminine person. They see my personality as masculine, and think of my skirts and heels as a form of drag. To me though, that doesn't really gel either. My femininity is just sort of my own mix. I'm incredibly independent and competent, but with sequins. Once we let go of the ideas that our gender or even just the way we present our gender has any bearing on what we should be doing in bed we can all start having more fun.

For some folks gender is a totally integral part of their personality. It's more than how they dress, it's also what turns them on and makes sex hot. For other folks it's more about aesthetic than it is about a bedroom role. And sometimes our gender doesn't line up with our biological sex and it prevents us from being able to fully relate to our bodies. Sometimes folks who have this experience will take hormones or have surgery so that the outward appearance lines up with the way they imagine themselves. But regardless of what our gender is, what we look like, what parts we are working with, or how we got them, we don't need to let some made-up idea of masculine and feminine dictate how we get off.

Once you start getting into bed with more than one person, especially if you are getting into bed with the same sex, gender is going to get more complicated. Think about the influence of gender in your own life. Is there a certain way of dressing that makes you feel sexy? One of the prime examples of gender's oppressive role in sex is the idea that being penetrated is a feminine trait and penetrating is a masculine one. Well, says who? This sad little idea is a big downer in your sex life. And it's especially annoying when you are having sex with multiple partners because worrying about what's appropriate behavior for your gender is only going to keep you from doing things you might enjoy.

> *I've always wanted to get fucked in the ass; but I feel weird asking my girlfriend to do it. My ideal threeway would involve my girlfriend fucking me with a strap-on while some other girl sat on my face.*
>
> —A

I'm not knocking gender roles. Feminine and masculine role-playing can be very hot and certainly have their place in your sex life. I'm just trying to remind you that masculine and feminine have nothing to do with your anatomy. Some of the hottest boys I've ever had sex with have had the same parts as I do. And here's a little known secret: I've turned more than one straight boy into a screaming girl.

Go ahead and add gender play to your threeway, strap it on and fuck someone if you've never done so. Or put on a nightie and throw your legs in the air if that's something you've never tried. Just don't get confused and think that what is between your legs dictates how you should get it on.

SEXUAL SELF-ESTEEM

> *As I've gotten older I've learned to enjoy sex more. I wouldn't go back to being twenty-one for anything.*
>
> —K, 37

•••

> *I know I'm good in bed. I might not have a perfect body, but I'm sure as hell a sex goddess.*
>
> —A, 32

How are you supposed to really enjoy sex if you are worried about how your body looks? Leave that low self-esteem at home. If you are sexually driven enough to want a threeway, then you are sexually sophisticated to know that confidence makes sex more enjoyable.

How Do We Become Confident?

First of all, identifying as a sexual person who deserves to have great sex is pretty key to your self-image. If you get caught up in the idea that only people with porn-star bodies have great sex, potential lovers will sense this about you and it will become a self-fulfilling prophecy. Be proactive about your desire. Chase the kind of sex you want. Chase the partners that get you all worked up. You are a hot fuck; commit it to memory.

Want to have more confidence in bed? Teach yourself about sex. Read more books like this one. Watch porn. Read erotica. Surf the Web. Talk to your partners. Pay attention. Most of us got a pretty lame sexual education as teens but were suddenly expected to be great lays as adults. It doesn't work that way. Great lovers are not born, they are made.

Practice, Practice, Practice.

Yes, I realize that's an obvious one. But the more sexual experience you gain the more confident you will be when it comes to getting your lovers off. This is a great reason to have threeways; you get to practice on more than one person at a time!

Be adventurous. Don't get yourself caught in sexual ruts. Try new things. The more you discover about your own sexuality, the more your self-esteem will get a boost.

Love your inner horndog. Masturbate frequently. Leave your inhibitions at home. Seek out others who are like you. Enjoy yourself.

So now you've learned all about sexual anatomy. You can name all the parts and what they do. Hopefully this information will help you out in your search for adventure. Now that you are a little more familiar with the terrain you can set out to have fun with any gender your horny little heart desires. In the next chapter we'll talk about some basic sex skills that will help boost your confidence in the sack and make you a better lover.

CHAPTER 6

BRUSH UP YOUR SEX SKILLS

ONE GREAT THING ABOUT multiple-partner sex is all the new sexual techniques and tricks you'll learn from the people you are crawling into bed with. And if you pay close attention your threeway can be an educational experience as well as fantasy fulfillment. If it's your first time it's normal to be a little nervous. If you are used to only dealing with one type of body and suddenly there's a whole new set of genitals in your face you might need a few pointers. And if you have suddenly found yourself in bed with a different gender than you are used to wrestling with, then everything is going to seem all that more intimidating. Hopefully this chapter will give you the confidence you need to rock your new playmates world.

Being completely comfortable with our sexuality isn't always the easiest thing. When we first start having sex, we don't necessarily feel entitled to sexual pleasure. In fact even as we get more experienced we don't really ever fully embrace the idea that we're entitled to a fab sex life. Many of us take our sex lives for granted. We forget to work on them. Or worse, if we aren't having a fantastic sex life we think maybe it's because we aren't desirable. Great sex takes a lot of work. Luckily the work is fun and the sex makes it all worth it.

ASK FOR WHAT YOU WANT IN BED

We all know by now that communication is the key to great sex. But how many of us are completely comfortable saying to our lovers "Baby, I want you to do this to me." Actually it was the great sexpert Susie Bright that once said "No one is ever going to be able to gaze into your eyes and tell how you want to get fucked in the ass." And ain't that the truth? Asking for what we want takes practice, and it also takes a certain type of sexual confidence that most of us aren't born with. But don't dismay, smart sexual communication can be learned. One of the reasons that most sex educators stress communication over specific sex tricks is that all bodies are different and none of us respond exactly the same way sexually. So you can have a million moves up your sleeve and still find yourself unable to set your lover's knickers on fire for the simple reason that you can't figure out what works best without a little feedback. But once you've learned how to communicate about sex, you can start changing up those tricks to suit whatever lucky duck happens to be in your bed.

More People to Please

One thing you will find when you enter the land of multiple-partner sex is that there are more people to please than you are used to. If you are half of a couple and used to having partner sex, then having a new person in your bed is going to add a whole new set of sexual hurdles. Alternatively, if you are mainly a solo player and you've suddenly got two people ready and willing, you'll need some pretty good communication skills to make sure everyone gets what they want. You suddenly have your own desire to navigate with two new people, and then the desire of two people who are used to getting each other off but for whom your body is foreign territory. No matter how you think about it.

A successful threeway takes work. Michael Smith, CEO of Tantus Silicone, says "A threeway with two women might be every man's fantasy, but if you want to do it right it takes a lot of planning." He's right. Sex rarely just happens. And if you expect it you are setting yourself up for disappointment.

Have a Plan

You should approach your threeway the same way you'd approach any other event: think it through and come up with a plan. You don't need a script, but a general idea of what you want combined with a good foundation that includes great sexual communication and an understanding that sex isn't magic and actually takes work will make it much more fun. Michael adds "It's not really about having two girls on one guy. It's about three people pleasing each other. And if that's the type of threeway you are involved in, then you have two women to please and you want to make sure everyone is emotionally satisfied as well as sexually satisfied. And it's tricky from a guy's standpoint because you essentially have one crack at getting off and you need to time it so that all of you are happy and you get to enjoy yourself."

It's Not About How You Look

We rely heavily on our visual sense during sex. And it's our visual sense that usually lands us in bed with someone in the first place. We see someone we find attractive, they find us attractive and the game is on. But in reality, having fantastic sex has nothing whatsoever to do with your appearance. Great sex and good communication come from having sexual self-confidence. And that confidence comes from practice and knowing yourself. Start out by masturbating and teaching yourself what you like. Realizing you are sexy and understanding how you work and what turns you on is far more valuable in the sack than having a huge dick or big porn star tits.

TALKING DIRTY MAKES YOU A BETTER LOVER

Talking dirty will make it easier to ask for what you want in bed. While it's important to have a vocabulary for sex outside of the bedroom, it's just as important to have a way to talk about sex that starts the little sex engines, or keeps them going when you are in the middle of sex.

Talking dirty will not only make it easier to ask your partner or partners for what you want in a way that turns them on, it will also give them the space to tell you what they like and don't like in an erotic context.

Sex Is in the Brain

Many of us find ourselves completely tongue-tied in bed. And if someone asks what we want we just mutter something about how it all feels good. But learning to use a sexual vocabulary makes it much sexier to say exactly what's on our minds. Talking dirty is really just sexual communication without any touchy feely New Age stuff that might turn some of us, myself included, off. It's sexual communication that's also sexy. Think of it as foreplay.

I use this technique with my lover all the time. I'll curl up next to her in bed and ask her to tell me what she's been fantasizing about, or what's she's jerked off to lately. And that conversation will start a dialogue that leads to sex. I like to plant ideas in her head about what I'd like to do in bed by telling her dirty things during the day and getting her worked up. And she does this with me as well. Sometimes I'll get a phone call, or even just a text message, with something so incredibly smutty in it that my concentration will be shot for a good portion of the day.

I think we drastically underrate the cerebral side of sex. Some of the hottest sex I've had in my lifetime consisted of me telling my lover a dirty fantasy while she jerked off. In our fantasies, anything can happen. We aren't limited by our physicality. We can play roles, play with age, play with different power dynamics, have multiple lovers, and all sorts of other things.

The Fantasy-Masturbation Exercise

Try this as an exercise to get used to talking about fantasies in bed. Go down to your local bookstore and pick out some erotica that interests both of you. Dress yourself in something sexy, light candles, dim the lights, or do whatever it is that usually gets you in the mood for sex. Crawl under the covers with your lover.

Start by reading an erotic story out loud. Just read it straight through without worrying about how you sound. If it gets you hot, great. If it just feels uncomfortable or embarrassing, that's OK, too.

If you feel like going on, read another story. This time try and relax into it, get more comfortable with the language. If you are generally pretty shy about sex talk and the story makes you uncomfortable, go ahead and laugh. Sometimes erotica is just funny. Avoid reading any stories that talk about beautiful love flowers or stamens or other bad floral metaphors.

Now, hand your lover a vibe if she's female or some really good lubricant designed for masturbation if he's male. You are going to talk about sex and your special friend should masturbate if they feel inclined or inspired by your story. Start out by describing thoughts you might have had during the day. Don't feel shy. This is a low-pressure exercise; you don't have to be totally comfortable right away.

If you are stuck for something to talk about, describe the most recent sex you've had together. Just describe what the two of you did. Tell your lover what parts you liked the most. Say things like "It was really hot when you had your mouth against my inner thigh," or "I loved feeling your hands all over my ass."

Pay attention to your lover's reactions when you say certain things. Positive feedback is the best training technique. If someone we are hot for gets excited by something we do, it makes us want to do it all the time. Stay aware of your partner and let yourself get turned on by his or her excitement.

Now that you've warmed up a little bit, try heading into fantasy territory. Describe a scenario, possibly a threeway scenario that gets you hot. Tell your lover exactly what you imagine him or her doing, describe the way it looks and the way it makes you feel. It's

OK to talk about things you might not actually feel comfortable doing in real life. That's what fantasy is for.

Encourage your partner to masturbate to climax. Just tell him or her to go for it. Get them off with your voice. Try and pay attention to how it feels to use language and intonation as a sexual tool. Build the intensity of your fantasy along with your lover's orgasm.

Did it work? Did you relax enough to talk your bed partner through an orgasm? If so, congratulations! If you felt too awkward or weird, that's OK. Rinse and repeat as necessary.

How to Talk Dirty

Plain old talking dirty is a little different than talking about your fantasies in bed. Sometimes we don't need the whole scenario, we might just need to be fucked, or stroked, or licked, or sucked harder or from a different angle. Maybe we just like the sound of certain words. Sometimes dirty talk is hot because it increases our brain/body connection. Describing the physical attention with dirty language can increase its intensity. Master the art of talking dirty and you can give your lover directions without having to stop the scene.

If you are normally silent in bed, start out your smut talk foray by making some noise. A few well-timed ooohhhs, aaahhhs, and OhMyGods can take you pretty far. Then try describing what your partner is doing to you as it's happening. "You are fucking me really hard," or "You are sucking my cock."

Ok, now add some pet names. Go ahead. Anything will work. Try baby, sugar, daddy, honey, officer, bastard, sir, lover, stud, slut, whore, or bitch (if you like that kind of thing—some perfectly reasonable folks think being called a cocksucking slut is the most romantic thing in the world).

The next step is to use some actual dirty words. No more talking about your *down there* and your *special purpose*. You've moved beyond that now. Get with the program.

Here are some dirty terms to use during sex

- For your lady parts: pussy, cunt, cooze, snatch, hole, chach, cooch, pie, box
- For your manly parts: prick, cock, dick, rod, pole, meat, stick
- For your butt: ass, crack, asshole, dirty star, back door, tail
- For intercourse: fuck, plug, ball, bang, shag, stick it
- For oral sex: eat out, go down on, lick, lap, blow job, suck

Now try stringing them all together and see what you get. Go on. Pick a pet name, an action term, and a body part, and make a sentence. You should come up with something pretty good. Next thing you know you'll be screaming "Fuck my hole you bitch" with the best of them. Just keep it down so you don't upset the neighbors.

HOW TO KISS

Kissing is the perfect seduction tool. Learn to kiss like a pro and you'll end up with a lot more lovers than friends. "I once had a threeway with two guys. One of them was a great kisser and would get me really turned on, and one of them was a terrible kisser and kept turning me off. So it was like being on a rollercoaster," says Jamye Waxman, *Playgirl* magazine.

Do's

1. LET THE ANTICIPATION BUILD. Rushing into a first kiss is the most common mistake lovers make. Flirt until the object of your affection is moving closer. And let him or her remain close even if it feels awkward or uncomfortable. Wait until the other person is practically begging.

2. BEGIN SOFTLY. Forget what you've read in romance novels and erotic thrillers, you aren't Rico Suave and all

that bodice-ripping is lame. Start out with a very slow, light kiss. No tongue in the beginning. Play with his or her lips a little. Suck and nibble them.

3. LET THE URGENCY FOR A DEEPER KISS BUILD, then give in to it. Explore his or her mouth with your tongue. Explore lips and teeth.

4. VARY YOUR TECHNIQUE. Switch between light, soft kisses and passionate, deeper ones. Kissing is like any other part of sex, so keep it interesting. Mix it up a bit. Kiss consciously; pay attention to what you are doing and your partner's responses.

5. TALK. Whisper sexy things in between kisses. Tell him or her how attractive they are. Talk about how you felt when you first saw them.

Don'ts

1. DON'T DROOL. Sloppy wet kisses aren't sexy.

2. DON'T JUST SHOVE YOUR TONGUE in his or her mouth. It's not a weapon.

3. DON'T TENSE UP. The best kisses come from soft, relaxed lips. A tense kiss can ruin the mood.

Once you've mastered the art of talking about what you want to do and what you want to have done to you, it's time to move on to working on your skill set. If you are entering into your first multiple-partner sexual experience it's entirely possible you'll be playing with bodies and genders you haven't had the opportunity to get sexual with before. Don't despair. You know how to talk about sex, so talk about it!

HOW TO GO DOWN ON A WOMAN

Oral sex is one of the most commonly fantasized about threeway sex acts. One of the benefits of having sex with more than one person is getting to experience oral sex from both sides of the equation simultaneously. Or to experience giving or receiving oral sex while also fucking or engaging in whatever other sex act turns you on. More survey respondents than I can even count mentioned that they wanted to perform cunnilingus on someone while also being penetrated or getting a blow job. From what I could tell, everyone wants to eat pussy. And many of the would-be bi ladies felt nervous about their first time going down. Relax, it's not that hard. But if you are new to it you just might need a few pointers.

I feel like this is the place for me to come out about the fact that I wrote a book on cunnilingus. Because I did. It's called *Box Lunch: The Layperson's Guide to Cunnilingus*. And it's great, of course. So when it comes to telling you how to eat pussy, I feel like I know what I'm talking about. Also, I'm a lesbian so that means I get to do it and get it done to me. Sometimes even at the same time. I think this gives me an advantage. And if you are a bi-curious chick who has never eaten pussy before, don't worry your pretty little head. You'll catch on quickly. We all have to start out somewhere.

The first thing you'll need to get through your head about giving head is that no two women are alike when it comes to getting off. There are some basic techniques you will probably want to master, but when it comes down to the getting off part you'll need to pay lots of attention to your lady's body language and verbal cues.

Start off slowly. Tease her and drag out the stimulation as long as you possibly can. We often use oral sex as a form of foreplay, but in my opinion that is jumping in too soon. Oral sex is sex, people! You wouldn't jump on the bed and start humping, would you? You'd engage in a little foreplay beforehand. Well, get her warmed up before you go south. Use your hands and voice, talk dirty, and caress her. Nibble her earlobes, pull her hair, give her a spanking. If she's shy about being gone down on in front of someone else, then make sure that person gets in on the action rather than just watching the show. The third party can distract the nice lady by making out with her, or maybe even climbing on her face depending on where the three of you are in your groove. Just make sure to give your lady friend plenty of time to get turned on. Warm her up. Do whatever you normally do to get in the mood. Then you can commence with the cunnilingus.

Working your way slowly down her body lets her know what's coming. Move from making out, to kissing her neck, to her abdomen and thighs, before getting anywhere near her vulva.

Nuzzle your face into her pubic hair (if she has any) and lightly lick the outside of her outer labia. Pay close attention to cues. If she's inching toward your face you are in good shape. Spread her thighs with your hands and press your lips against her labia. Hold still and let her feel the build of anticipation. You can lightly lick between her lips at this point, or continue to torture her as long as you feel necessary.

Now, work your tongue between her labia and lick up toward the top of her mons until you feel her erect clit. Work your tongue up and down from the tip of her clit to the bottom of her vagina. A wide flat tongue works great for this. Do this lightly for as long as you like. The heat and pressure from your mouth should feel wonderful to her by now, but you are just getting started so continue to move slowly. Switch between a wide flat tongue and a relaxed tongue. Move languidly around her entire vulva letting her feel the pressure of your tongue.

The first few tentative licks are my favorite part of cunnilingus. The minute my partner's warm tongue makes contact with my clit I go a little crazy. It's really a sensation that I can't get enough of. Draw it out in the beginning. This serves two purposes. It allows her time to get hot and bothered and it lets her know you aren't in a hurry. The last thing you want is for her to think she needs to hurry up and come. Make appreciative moans and show her just how happy you are to be between her thighs.

When you think you have her sufficiently warmed up you can begin to pay more attention to her clit. Try different tongue positions and shapes. A hard pointed tongue is very useful for making small, tight circles around her clit, a softer tongue can lick up and down over her clit and hood. Start with one technique and switch to the other after a few minutes. With pussy-eating it's important to build up a rhythm but not to stay in the same rhythm so long that she gets bored. Saliva is your friend here. She's probably plenty wet by this point, but the wetter the better. So use your tongue to spread the love around.

Take brief little breaks from the clit every few minutes and travel around to the rest of her coochie. A light fluttering busy little tongue is going to keep her very happy. Lick her inner labia, and toy around with the opening to her vagina. Tease it lightly with your tongue and penetrate her with an in-and-out motion. But don't stray from the clit for too long. Really her clit is where you want to pay most of your attention. But moving away from it and coming back will build the tension without overstimulating her. If you concentrate on the clit too soon it's possible she'll get worked up but not be able to go the distance. So dance around her clit and all over her vulva until she's at the breaking point.

Perhaps now it's time to employ the fingers? When the pussy-licking starts getting hot and heavy you might want to spread apart her outer labia with your fingers to get more access to her sensitive clit. This has the added effect of pulling back her clitoral hood and exposing her mini hard-on in all its glory. You can also stick two fingers in her pussy and stimulate her G spot with a come-hither motion. Getting your fingers and tongue into a groove and working together is a surefire crowd pleaser.

You may also want to try playing lightly with her butthole. Use a very wet finger to lightly rim the outside of her anus. If she responds favorably to this then try lightly penetrating her hole a little bit at a time. Go slowly and make sure your fingers are very wet with her juices and saliva. And don't penetrate her with more than the very tip of your finger without adding a commercial lubricant. There are many lubes that have no taste and smell and won't ruin the fun during cunnilingus. Even if she's responding eagerly, don't just go sticking things in there. A little careful butt play never hurt anyone. If she's nervous about it then you'll want to move extra slowly and gently. But if you pay attention and don't rush in you may just find that the way to her O is through her ass.

Most women orgasm in response to direct rhythmic clitoral stimulation. If you've gotten her close, which you should be able to judge by her body language and the sounds she's making, then you can start concentrating all your attentions on her clit. Find a beat and stick to it. Small little circles around alternated with big loopy circles work nicely. So does a side-to-side move mixed in with an up-and-down one. Whatever you pick, stay with it and go the distance. You can switch between just moving your tongue and moving your jaw and head when your tongue begins to tire.

If she starts pulling your hair and pushing your face into her pussy, you're doing a great job. Just be careful, I've had a few enthusiastic lovers in my life go crazy and nearly suffocate me while they were getting off. I'm perfectly happy to risk death to make a lady feel good, but if you end up blacking out before she finishes coming, she won't have much of an orgasm.

After she climaxes, keep your tongue on her clit. You might be able to extend her orgasm this way. Sometimes women are too sensitive postcome for this. But a little pressure applied with a still flat tongue can feel wonderful. Try it out and see how it goes.

HOW TO GO DOWN ON A MAN

Most of the men I spoke with for this book felt that blow jobs were really a perfect anytime activity. One guy said "Why keep it for special occasions? I like BJs during lunch, at the aquarium, while driving, in line at the bank, wherever." But the reason fellatio lends itself so well to a threeway is that it leaves your hands and mouth free to please someone else. You can be getting the best head of your life and still have enough tools at your disposal to rock someone else's world.

It might seem easy, but there's more to a blow job than merely bobbing your head up and down over your lover's cock. If you take cues from the way your lover moves and you understand that men, like women, all work differently and respond to stimulation in various ways then there's no reason you can't become a cock-sucking master. If you've never been up close and personal with a man's genitals go back and reread the chapter on anatomy. Get yourself familiar with all the different parts and then come back and test drive your ideas.

The one rule to keep in mind is "Don't bite." While all men are different, no one wants teeth marks on their willy. If you are a gay girl who's mainly been around the detachable variety of dick, then you'll find you need to be a bit gentler with the flesh and blood type. Also, because bio-cocks are often smaller and softer than dildos they are a lot easier to maneuver. Tricks like deep throating will be a whole lot easier on a real cock than they would be on a strap-on.

If you are a straight man and you've never really gotten busy with your own kind before, then just relax and think about all the fun things you've liked people to do to you in the past. Work from there. While it won't tell you everything you need to know, a little trip down memory lane will certainly help you get comfortable with the cock in your face.

Cocks, like pussies, have more sensitive parts and less sensitive parts. And just like with pussy-eating, your best bet is to concentrate your tongue work on the more sensitive parts of the penis.

Start slowly. Just because he has a raging hard-on doesn't mean he wants you to attack his schlong like it's an oxygen mask and you are underwater. Use your hands to stroke it. Grasp and squeeze the shaft. Play with his balls. Run your fingers underneath his balls and stroke his perineum.

Try running your tongue along the glans or head of the penis. The outer coronal ridge is sensitive and responds nicely to gentle licking and sucking. The raphe, or the ridge on the underside of the dick is the most sensitive part of the shaft. You can concentrate tongue work on that spot, but for the most part when it comes to the shaft you'll make everyone happier by wrapping your mouth around it and pumping your head up and down. You can use your hand as an extension of your mouth, wrapping your fist around his dick and then following the movement of your mouth with your hand. Paying a lot of tongue attention to the head and ridge and sensitive frenulum (the sensitive spot underneath, remember your anatomy lesson?) and then using your hand to pump up and down the shaft feels good to both the licker and lickee.

Sucking his dick puts you in an excellent position to explore as much of his genital region as you can reach. Don't forget to pay attention to his balls and inner thighs. You can also try teasing the crack of his ass and maybe lightly stroking his anus with your fingers. If he responds well to having his butthole stimulated, try lubing up a finger and slowly penetrating him. Try sucking his cock while your other lover plays with his ass and balls. Or two of you can take turn sucking his dick like a Popsicle. Be creative.

Try getting as much of his cock down your throat as you can.

While deep throating lacks the finesse of tongue action around his head, it looks very impressive and the visual kick is enough to make it a worthy goal. Deep throating is much easier if you relax. If you gag a bit, don't panic. Gagging is a natural reaction to having something block your throat. Make an effort to relax your throat. Your partner should let you lead in this case. And only take as much at a time as you are comfortable with. Wrap your hand around the base of his cock to prevent it from going in any farther than you are comfortable with. Practice swallowing his cock until you feel comfortable, then go the distance. There are a few positions that work well for deep-throating, and in porn flicks they always seem to be lying on a bed with their head thrown over the edge. This seems too complicated, if you ask me. I recommend experimenting until you find a position you feel comfortable in.

> *I love giving head. It's my favorite thing to do. I had a threeway with my boyfriend and another girl and we took turns blowing him. She'd suck his cock for a while, and then I'd suck it, and in between we'd stop and make out. It was heavenly!*
>
> —J, 26

Another neat trick is to lie back passively and let your partner fuck your mouth as if it were your pussy or ass. This game works well during sex that involves power play. While technically it's probably less fun for the suckee than putting their all into giving great head, it's a very mentally stimulating act. Sometimes it's fun to feel used and abused, or like you are simply a tool for your partner's pleasure. Try kneeling in front of your lover while he uses your hair to pull your head back. Allow him to fuck your mouth, but make sure he knows how far he can push his cock in without gagging you! Talk about it beforehand and if his cock is very large ask him to wrap his hand around the base of the shaft. Gagging can be very hot, and it gives the top a sense of power. But it's only a fun part of sex play when everyone agrees to it.

> *I've had all kinds of threeways but my favorite threeway was with two guys. I picked them both up at a bar one night when I was feeling especially bold. They'd both been flirting with me and buying me drinks and I finally realized I was going to have to choose which one got to go home with me when one of them, let's call him B, suggested the three of us all leave together. We went to B's place and had a few more drinks and talked and finally B put on a porno. I figured what the hell and just went with it. It wasn't long before we were all naked. I started giving B a blowjob while guy number 2, let's call him S, was fingering my pussy. I was so turned on and wet and I could barely stand it. At first I was a little at a loss about what to do with both of them, but we kind of got into a rhythm and just sort of took turns with each other. At one point I was making out with S while B was going down on me, that was really great. I had the most amazing orgasm of my life that night, probably more because the whole situation was so hot than because either of them was particularly skilled.*
>
> —L, 28

BEND-OVER BOYFRIENDS AND DICK-WIELDING CHICKS

Oh, the strap-on. It's a much beloved tool among the dyke set, but its popularity has been rapidly growing among the straight but not narrow crowd. "Over the past couple of years I've seen a dramatic increase in hetero couples excited to explore female-male penetration. Prostate awareness has been growing in the medical industry, and it's nice to see that couples are looking for ways to find pleasure in something that's also an important part of their sexual awareness," says Coyote Days, the senior sex toy buyer for Good Vibrations, a major sex toy retailer.

In my humble yet professional opinion, a threeway is the time for the strap-on to shine. Depending what gender combo meal you've ordered an extra cock might be the perfect side dish. And even if you've got more cocks than you know what to do with, a strap-on will come in handy when one or the other of you is resting in preparation for another round.

Some straight men quake in fear at the prospect of sticking something up their asses. If this is you, please go back to chapter three and reread the section on gender and anatomy. Get over the idea that female-bodied people are fuckees and male-bodied people are fuckers and you'll start having a lot more fun in bed. If you are a chick who has never strapped it on before I'd bet you'll find having a silicone hard-on a pretty exciting thing. You may notice in the beginning that it throws off your center of balance. If you've always been a receptive partner, thinking of your pelvis in this new way takes some getting used to. If you feel silly, go with it. Don't be shy, play around with your new cock, wear it around the house, do the dishes in it if you must. Everyone feels awkward at first. Don't worry. Wear that baby until it begins to feels like a part of you. You'll eventually see how delightful a silicone dick can be.

Owning a strap-on really expands the options of your threeway. You can fuck your best friend while someone watches. You can do your boyfriend in the butt while he goes south on another girl. You can get a blowjob from one person while giving a blowjob to another. The combinations are endless.

The anal taboo is pretty powerful, and anyone who's willing to offer up their ass for penetration gets a big gold star in the sex department. Free your mind and your ass will follow, that's what I always say.

I'm a woman who loves to penetrate my boyfriend while I give him head. I usually use a small butt plug and push it in and out while I am blowing him. He comes so hard when I do this to him.

—V, 23

Now, for the fun part: what to do with it.

A staggering number of the folks I interviewed for this book were into a little bend-over boyfriend action. Seriously, one out of every three threeway tales involved the boyfriend or husband getting bent over and done with a dick. I'm not sure if that's because I interviewed mainly sexually adventurous couples or if it's truly a widespread trend. But if you aren't doing it, you are missing out. Imagine going south on your girlfriend while a hot chick pokes your prostrate with a silicone strap-on. Ah, sounds like multiple orgasms to me!

If you are a man who wants to be penetrated anally, talk to your partner about it. If your threeway involves someone who knows his or her way around a dildo, then you're in luck. But if you all happen to be dildo virgins then here are a few tips to help you out.

You'll want a silicone dildo and a harness. The harness should be practical and comfortable but it doesn't have to be a huge investment. A company called Sportsheets makes a great line of inexpensive strap-on harnesses that are designed for couples into this kind of play. Anything from their line should work out just fine.

There are a million reasons to buy silicone sex toys but the most important one is probably that silicone is sterilizable. You can boil it, you can bleach it, you can put it in the dishwasher. If you are buying a dick to use in your threeway, more than one party may use it. While you should be putting condoms on all of your sex toys anyway, you'll still want to sterilize your dick when the party is over. Also, cheaper dildos are made of unstable rubbers and plastics that do something called outgassing. This means the chemicals are leaking out of them. You know that plastic smell you get when you open the package? That's chemicals leaking out of the toy. Do you really want to put those chemicals in your body? I didn't think so.

Your eyes are probably bigger than your ass. Start out with something small. Do a little research online. Try reading up about dildos on Web sites like Blowfish.com, Babeland.com, and goodvibes.com. Play around with fingers until you have a good idea of how much you actually want going up your butt. Dildos come in every size from pinky finger to traffic cone. Pick wisely and your new toy will last a long, long time.

If you'll be wearing the cock, you might want to look into the many options for getting a little stimulation while you are on the business end. Some cocks come with a hole in the base that holds a small vibe, giving the wearing a little zing. There are also a few well-designed double dildos on the market, the best being something called the Feeldoe. It's a patented design created by a woman to use on her partners. Most major sex-toy retailers carry it. Check the resource section for ideas about where to shop.

Wearing a strap-on dick allows you to step away from the idea that women are naturally the receptive partner. You'll feel powerful and hot. Go with that. Really advanced players learn to create a mind-body connection and embrace their "psychic cock." The dildo may not have any nerve endings, but it sure as hell works as a powerful representation of the hard-on you have going on in your head. Embrace your dick, get comfortable with it, and you may find eventually that you can climax from penetrating your partner with it. Practice, practice, practice. It's a neat trick that many dykes and transmen I know have mastered. Who cares if during the day you're a soccer mom? You can still have a hardon, baby.

How to Suck Detachable Dick

One fun thing about strap-ons is that they allow you to treat your female partner to a blow job. Silicone BJs are fun for everyone. The wearer gets a great show, the suckee gets the thrill of having his or her mouth penetrated and of being watched, and person number three gets to watch and possibly join in. It's sexy, it's genderbending, and it's even a little bit dirty. If you are a guy and you've never sucked a cock, I strongly suggest you get down on your knees right now and give a nice long loving blow job to your female lover.

1. PUT ON A SHOW. Your playmate is getting off by watching you. Lick, suck, and caress the dildo with a lot of showy movements. Because we are dealing more with indirect stimulation than nerve endings, you can do a lot of fancy tongue maneuvers that might not work on a biocock.

2. USE YOUR HAND to push the base of the dick into his or her cunt as you suck it. The receiver is going to get the most physical sensation from the point where the base of the dildo touches his or her body. Work your hand around the cock and grind it against the wearer's pelvis as much as you can.

3. NO IT ISN'T REAL. But it can certainly feel that way to the wearer. So try some of the tricks you'd normally use on a biocock. Deep throat it, lick the balls, run your tongue around the glans and coronal ridge.

When my female lover sucks me off she looks like a hot fag boy. I love watching her on her knees. It gives me days of fantasy material afterwards. I like jacking off thinking about my dirty girl-boy on her knees.

— N, 36

•••

I had a threeway with a married couple and the woman had never been fisted before, so I fisted her while he watched. And then after I was done, I fucked him while she watched. I had two fingers in his ass, and then three, and then I had nearly my entire hand in his ass and his wife was fascinated. She asked him if he realized how many fingers I had in him and I assured her that he was well aware of just how deep I was fucking him.

—M, 40

•••

I want to give my lover a lap dance and striptease but I feel shy about it. I'm afraid I won't be very graceful and she won't really enjoy it. Sometimes I think about giving head to one of her friends while she watches. I think it would be really exciting to have her friend's strap-on in my mouth. I would put on a really good show. That's really the trick to dyke blow jobs, you have to be into putting on a good performance. I mean, it's a dildo and as much as a lot of women I know treat it like it is real, it still doesn't have nerve endings. So I like to pay very close attention to all of my movements. I've practiced a lot and I know how to swing my hair around and do all sorts of showy things with my tongue so that the other person really gets off on the visuals. But it would be extra hot to be watched by another person while I gave head. I think they'd get really into it, but since they weren't the one getting the blow job they could concentrate more fully on what I was doing and how sexy I looked. I've brought this up once or twice during sex as part of a fantasy, but I haven't really made

> *it clear that I want to do it in real life. I'm waiting for my partner to get so turned on by the idea that she brings it up herself.*
>
> —S, 34

FISTING 101

If you are a female-bodied person who normally sleeps with men, there will probably be many new and exciting sex practices you'll discover by sleeping with chicks. But there's one thing in particular that you can really only do with another woman and that's fisting.

Fisting is the practice of inserting an entire hand into a vagina, and it's not as hard as it sounds. Often times intense finger fucking will naturally evolve into fisting, because during arousal the back two-thirds of the vagina balloon out in a process called "tenting," making enough room for a fist. This can be an intense activity, though it's perfect for a threeway as one partner can hold the fistee and help her relax while the fister works her magic. Before you even think about fucking a woman this way make sure your nails are all trimmed to the quick and filed smooth. This is good manners for having sex with girls anyway, but for fisting it's essential. Latex gloves will make this a safe activity, but they can also help to make your hand more slippery and easier to slide in.

Fisting is a slow process, but oh is it ever worth it. Assuming you've been doing whatever it takes to get warmed up and your lady is already on her back and begging for action, start by fucking her with a couple of fingers. Slowly work your way up to four fingers, adding lots of lube along the way. If she's turned on enough for a fist you'll know it. She'll feel open and receptive and you'll begin to feel like it's actually possible to slip your hand in there.

When she's comfortable with four fingers, add more lube to your hand and then curl your thumb into your palm to form a duckbill shape. Rotating back and forth slightly at the entrance of her vag will help open her up for what's to come.

As you push into her vagina your hand will begin to naturally ball into a fist. It may take a little maneuvering, work slowly.

Once you are inside, hold still and let her get used to the sensation of being filled up in this way. When she's ready you can begin to make subtle movements. Add lube liberally and often. Check in with her often. When she's ready for harder fucking she will let you know.

She may climax or not. If she does, her muscle contractions will probably push your hand out while she comes. Sometimes the experience of being fucked this way is too overwhelming to give her an orgasm. If she doesn't want to come, slowly withdraw your hand when she's ready for you to do so. Never pull out suddenly, even if her husband comes home early.

Hold her. Caress her. Take care of her. Fisting can be a very emotional experience.

•••

Now you're a pro. We've covered a lot of sexual ground in this chapter. And it's possible that a few of these ideas are totally new territory. But with all these new sex skills and your polished-up smut vocabulary you should be all set to get what you want out of your next threeway. In the next chapter we'll talk about sex toys, erotic massage, and spanking.

CHAPTER 7

ADVANCED TRICKS

THERE ARE SO MANY things to do in bed that we couldn't possibly cover them all. But now that you've gotten a handle on some basic threeway sex acts let's move on to some other fun things to do in bed with two or more willing partners. The first thing we will discuss is sex toys. Sex toys can really enhance a threeway. With all those extra holes and hands and mouths you might need more than your natural born parts to keep everyone busy. I'll also cover erotic massage, which technically isn't so much an advanced activity as it is something extra and a good way to break the ice with a new partner. Next we will look at spanking, which happens to be my favorite sexual activity of all time; and we'll wind it all up with talk about role-playing and safer sex.

THE WELL-STOCKED SEX TOY BOX

Good quality sex toys are one of the wonderful advances of the modern world. And the Internet, bless its easily accessible heart, makes sex toys easy to get and even easier to learn how to use. Nothing says prepared for a threeway, fourway, or more way romp like a well-stocked toy box.

While your sex toy box should be well stocked, it doesn't actually have to be a box. It can be a drawer in your nightstand, a shelf, or anything that works. My ex-girlfriend kept hers on a shelf above the bed, which seemed practical until the day we accidentally knocked a dildo out the window and it stood at attention like a little silicone soldier on the sidewalk. Someone happened to be moving into the building that day and the movers assumed they'd dropped it. After a lot of uncomfortable joking around, they scooped it up and stuck it in one of the boxes. Needless to say, we didn't ask for it back.

A well-planned toy collection shows your partners you care about their pleasure. If you're on a budget, start with the basics. Gather some safer sex supplies. You'll want some cheap condoms to keep toys clean, and better quality condoms for the penis in your life. You'll also want latex gloves and dental dams or a roll of plastic wrap for safer rimming and cunnilingus. And don't forget the lube! There are so many lube options available now it can be hard to choose, but stocking up on sample sizes of several different choices is the best way to always have the right lube around for the job. If anyone of your partners has an allergy or sensitivity to a lube ingredient, having a wide selection will save the day.

SOME THINGS YOUR TOY BOX MIGHT CONTAIN:

- A strong, small vibrator and a good firm silicone dildo, especially one with a G spot curve, will take you far in a multiple partner romp. A curved dildo can hit the prostate if you are of the male-bodied variety, and your G spot if you are female bodied. Some dildos even have a hollowed out base that fits a vibe, so you can poke, prod, and vibrate all at once. Fancy! To reiterate what we said in the last chapter, stick with silicone for insertable toys. It's boilable and nonporous—which means you can sterilize it.
- Glass and acrylic, however, are also fabulous. And a few companies are making impressive looking toys in stainless steel. Metal, glass, and acrylic toys are investments but will last forever. You can be buried with your dildo like Tutankhamen if it turns you on. These materials become super slippery with lube and the extra slick surface cuts down on friction soreness, meaning you get to play longer.

- Bullet vibrators are very handy; you can use them externally or slip them into a condom and put them in any hole you like. Just make sure to pull them out by the condom and not the cord.
- Dual-action vibes, like the Rabbit Vibe, have two components that move independently. The rotating shaft stimulates your G spot while the fluttering ears tickle your clit. This type of toy is more of a luxury item than a basic, but depending on your preferences you might want to move it onto the basics list.
- Butt plugs and bead toys are fun for everyone. Pop in a plug for a hands-free way to stimulate one partner anally while fucking another partner with your dildo or cock. Try pressing a vibrator to the base of a silicone butt plug—silicone transmits vibrations very well. Anal beads and toys shaped like strings of beads are super-duper orgasm enhancers. And they come in all sizes. Start with something petite; you can always size up. Remember: use liberal amounts of lube on any toy that's inserted anally. Also, all anal toys should have a flared base. Otherwise you might end up with an embarrassing emergency room story.
- Nipple clamps are fun. They look nice and kinky but are also a pragmatic way to stimulate someone's nips while your hands are busy elsewhere.
- You'll also want some bondage basics. If you are new to this kind of play start with a blindfold and a set of comfy restraints with Velcro closures. Blindfolding your lover is the easiest form of sensory deprivation, heightening your partner's sense of anticipation and vulnerability. Restraints make your bottom feel delightfully helpless, and the fact that he or she can't run away is just an added bonus.
- Spanking is the most familiar form of SM play. And a paddle will come in handy when your hand gets tired. Paddles are

sexy and a wielding one is a great way to intimidate your date. Try using the paddle, the restraints, and the blindfold all together when you want to really impress!

EROTIC MASSAGE

A good erotic massage is an all-encompassing sexual experience. It relaxes your partner, turns them on, gets them off and is just about guaranteed to make little cartoon hearts pop out of his or her eyes for weeks to come. It's a fun playtime experience for threeway sex because you have one person to receive the massage, one person to give it, and one person to facilitate and make sure the experience is perfect. It's a whole body-arouser and deeply sexual experience. The three of you can trade off receiving rubdowns, or designate roles to all involved parties. If you opt for a two-person massage, you'll have an extra set of hands, allowing you to make your lucky recipient feel loved, pampered, and overwhelmed by sensations.

An erotic massage is not just your average rubdown with almond oil and Yanni playing in the background. This particular type of massage ends with a *full release* as they say in the business (also known as a happy ending). The trick here is to build the intensity of touch, stroke by stroke, using all the tricks you have up your sleeve, until your lover is a little pile of turned-on goo. Then get them off in whichever manner they prefer.

Gather Your Tools

You'll need a few supplies for this activity, so plan ahead. Gather clean hand towels, massage oil, lube, candles, and a few of your lover's favorite sex toys. Recommended sex toys include: a dildo with a G spot curve, a pocket rocket, anal beads, a silicone butt plug, a slim, straight dildo for anal penetration, latex gloves, and condoms. If you are giving this massage on the floor you will want a cushy workout mat as well. You may also want some wine, bottled water, and light snacks for after. It's important to have everything within easy reach so that there's no need to break the mood. You don't want anyone to have to pad off to the kitchen. After this kind of intense sexual experience it's nice for all three of you to be able to relax in postcoital glow.

Dress Up

This is *erotic* massage people, so dress the part. Dressing for sex is an underrated activity. Nothing gets me in the mood like dressing up for my lovers. Dress up for your massage. If you are the recipient, you'll be naked of course. However the other two of you should go all out. For ladies, lingerie is always appropriate. Go extra racy; choose something shiny, crotchless, glittery, or trimmed with marabou; if it lights up or moves around on it's own, even better. For men, try sexy boxer shorts and a white tank, or maybe sexy special occasion underwear and a robe. If it were me receiving the massage I'd want my partner wearing boxer shorts and electrical tape on her nipples. Actually, I want her wearing that all the time. So maybe base your outfit on that.

Set the Scene

This isn't a quickie on the kitchen table kind of sex activity. It requires a little prep work. First, decide where you'll be giving the massage. Since you probably don't have a massage table in your house, and a bed is too bouncy for real massage, setting up a cozy little mat on the floor is one option. Futons also work well. Essentially what you want is a comfy but firm surface that allows you easy access to your lover's bod. Cover whatever surface you've decided on with clean towels and place a few extra hand towels within easy reach for wiping up oil and lube. Light candles. Maybe burn some incense. Crank up the heat. Put on sexy music; my favorite is any seventies R&B, especially Ohio Players. But go with what works for you. Avoid anything New Agey, and no Enya, unless you actually like that sort of thing.

Be a Giver

You want to make the evening special, so don't just blurt out "Hey, I want to rub your naked body and then masturbate you to orgasm!" Instead, surprise your lucky massagee by leading him or her blindfolded into the cozy little erotic massage love den you've created. The sex toys should all be displayed nicely in plain sight, perhaps lined up on a clean towel. But don't point them out. Don't forget to tease and draw out the excitement. Ply him or her with wine, and maybe some chocolates to get the mood flowing. Then either or both of you can dash into the bathroom like Clark Kent and change into your specially chosen sexy superhero massage outfit. The two of you can strip your lover slowly and lead him or her down onto the massage mat. He or she should start out lying face down. The room should be warm and comfortable.

Start Slowly

Pour some oil into your palm and rub your hands together to warm it. Begin with the mid-back using long firm strokes to soothe sore muscles. You don't need to be a massage therapist—any type of intimate touch is going to feel good. But pay attention to your movements, don't be sloppy or fast. Think of your actions as foreplay. Rub your hands up and down your lover's back, stopping to apply extra pressure anywhere you feel tension. Think of the mid-back as the center of the body, and work your way outward from there. Rub his or her shoulders and work your way down the arms. Then do the buttocks and work your way down the legs. Apply more oil as you go so that there is very little drag on the skin. If two of you are giving the massage, one person should work the top half of the body and the other should stay below the waist. Work to sync your movements.

Get to the Good Parts

As you massage your lover, pay special attention to his or her erogenous zones. This activity is a combination of massage and teasing. As you rub the mid-back, lightly graze the sides of the breasts. Tell her how beautiful she is. Work very slowly and don't be shy about vocalizing your enjoyment of her body as you touch her. Talk dirty if your partner finds that exciting (and really, who doesn't?). Rub her butt and slip your hand down between her cheeks and lightly stroke her anus and vulva. Add more oil to your hand and very lightly penetrate her anus. Rub the backs of her thighs in a kneading motion, moving her legs further apart. With a male partner, stroke the small of the back and buttocks. Slip your hand between his cheeks and graze his anus and perineum. Stroke the underside of the testicles. Do not speed up, and do not concentrate solely on the genitals. Make sure to incorporate the rest of the back and legs.

Now Do the Front

Ask your relaxed little horndog to turn over. Then kneel behind him or her cradling the head in your hands. Rub the neck with firm stokes as if you were lightly pulling her head away from her body. Place her head gently back on the pillow and work your way down the arms making sure to knead gently all the way to the ends of the fingers. Then slowly work your way across the torso gently stroking her breasts and stomach. Work across the hips. Lightly graze the genitals. Stroke his penis a few times, or lightly drag your fingers across your female lover's clit. Continue to work your way down the body to the feet, massaging and kneading the bottom of the foot and pulling gently at each toe.

Work Your Way Up Again

Once you are done with the feet it's time to work your way back up the legs. Knead your partner's body slowly, staying with your massage rhythm and push the legs apart as you rub her or him. Massage the insides of the thighs for as long as you both can stand it. Are you talking dirty? You should be. Hopefully at this point you've built your lover up to a fever pitch of arousal and she's dying for release. If your lover enjoys anal penetration, you may want to turn him or her back over at this point. If you are going for a straight-up hand job then face-up is fine. Wipe the oil off your hands with a towel and squirt some lube into your palm. Stroke the erect penis or clit, *communicate*, ask them how it feels and what they would like next.

The Happy Ending

Now it's time to employ the sex toys. What happens next depends on you and your partner's sexual preferences. He or she may want oral sex, or might want you to continue your handiwork. Another suggestion is to hand your female lover a small vibrator (like a pocket rocket) while you penetrate her with your fingers or a dildo. If she's an ejaculator, use the dildo with the G spot curve. If she's not an ejaculator, a curved dildo might make her into one. Your male lover might enjoy a lubed-up hand job with the addition of anal beads or a butt plug. Actually, your female lover might enjoy that, too. Go with what feels good and gets everyone off. It's a special occasion, so experiment with new toys and techniques. Afterwards, keep the energy going by showering together to wash off all the massage oil. Then the three of you can either switch roles, or just crawl into bed and have raucous sex for the rest of the night.

KINK: IT'S GOOD, CLEAN FUN

What makes sex great? According to the pervy types I interviewed for this book great sex requires a couple of open-minded partners who are willing to experiment, some taboo breaking, and some new tricks, new toys, and new faces. So in the interest of breaking some taboos and learning some new tricks, let's talk about a little light

BDSM. In the movies the kinky person is usually the bad guy. Or at least the mysterious person you should watch out for. Think of Madonna pouring candle wax on Willem Dafoe in *Body of Evidence*, or actually don't think of that. That movie was wretched.

BDSM stands for Bondage and Discipline, Domination and Submission, and Sadomasochism, and it can take your sex life from alright to *wow!* if you do it right. Get over your hang-ups. If you really think kink is weird you've watched too many episodes of *Law & Order*.

There are many reasons to bring a little bend into your sex life. Some people get off on bossing their lovers around; sometimes they find they really like being hit with a riding crop. Whatever it is that turns you on, embrace it. There are no rules, remember? Pleasure is good for you. And it's a lot more fun to play prison gang bang with three people than two.

Power Play

Playing with power roles is more than just being the sexual aggressor. If you are the "Top" you get total control of the scene. And if you are the "bottom" you give up all control and submit to your top's desires. One of my favorite ways to have a threeway is when my girlfriend and I have sex with a submissive third party. I like using the third person as a sexual catalyst. A willing and eager bottom brings a lot of excitement to a threeway. I can boss her around. I can ask her to masturbate while I watch, or force her to submit to my girlfriend's every whim. I get all the fun of having control and I get to watch everything that happens, thus engaging my bossy nature and voyeuristic side all at once. Heavenly!

There are lots of ways to get off on this kind of play. Maybe two of you would like to tie up the third person and force him or her to watch you have sex? Maybe the bottom has been very, very bad and needs a good spanking? Two of you can play harem slaves and submit to the desires of your controlling master. Or you can tie someone up and leave them there while the other two of you go get Chinese food. The possibilities are endless.

Safe Words

In a BDSM scene, "no" may sometimes mean "yes," "stop" can mean "don't stop," and "that hurts" can mean, "I'm going to come." The best way to negotiate this somewhat confusing syntax problem is to designate a safe word. When the bottom or sometimes the top uses the safe word it means the scene gets stopped, no questions asked. Your safe word can be anything, but one common trick is to use red, yellow, and green to control the intensity of what you are doing. Red means stop immediately, yellow means slow down it's getting too intense, and green means I'm OK, start back up again.

Bondage Basics

The best way to get someone to give up all control is to tie them up and maybe gag them. Then what are they gonna do about it, huh? But seriously, using restraints is one of the simplest ways to turn your sex life up a notch.

Remember the early nineties when Prince wanted out of his contract with Warner Bros. and went around in chains with the word slave written on his face? Well actual BDSM is way less ridiculous than that.

I have a friend who has a thing for zip ties, you know those plastic things the cops use to handcuff protestors so they can abuse them? She thinks they're sexy. I've been in a few too many protests to agree. To each his own. But the thing we do agree on is that restraining your sex partners is fun.

Safe Restraint

Restraining someone with something you cannot easily undo is dangerous and stupid. Stick with things that come off easily.

Anything that buckles is practical and so are Velcro cuffs, and Sportsheets makes an entire line of easy-to-use kits for bondage beginners. Rope is pretty and cheap, but the knots can be difficult to undo. And definitely avoid scarves and neckties. I don't care how many episodes of the *Red Shoe Diaries* you've masturbated to, typing up lovers with scarves is unsafe. The knots pull too tight and can't be undone without cutting. Stick with things that are designed for this kind of play.

Sensation Play and Sensory Deprivation

The other two fun little sex games that fall under the BDSM umbrella are sensation play and sensory deprivation. Sensation play means exactly what it sounds like: Playing with sensations. The sensations don't have to be painful, either. Remember *9 1/2 Weeks*? Well, Mickey Rourke did his BDSM basics homework and knew that an ice cube properly applied can be a pretty wonderful sex toy. Alternating between hot and cold, scratchy and soft, or stingy and dull are all ways to play with sensation. Try applying Tiger Balm and then ice, or dripping hot wax onto your partner's skin. A note about hot wax: beeswax melts at too high a temperature, but regular old household candles will work fine. The higher you hold the candle above your partner's body, the more time the dripping wax will have to cool before it hits the skin. Be smart. Test hot candle wax on your inner arm before you go near your lover.

Sensory deprivation, i.e., taking away one or more of their senses, will make anything you do to your partner seem more intense. In other words, I can see you but you can't see me.

Hopefully what you are doing to them feels good, or at least feels bad in a way that one of you is getting off on it. Things you can deprive your lover of sensation with include blindfolds, ear muffs, gags, and gas masks—if you are serious about this stuff, or just really weird. A blindfold is the most common form of sensory deprivation. Try making your partner wear one while you go down on him or her.

GIVE A GOOD SPANKING

Admit it. Every once in a while we all need a good spanking. Spanking is one of those fun but a little intimidating activities that everyone eventually embraces. And in a multiple-party scene, spanking is extra fun, because one of you can do the spanking, and one of you gets to hold him down.

I remember teaching one of my lovers to spank me. She was a good midwestern girl and nervous about anything she thought of as vaguely kinky. So I coaxed her into it by lying facedown on the bed with my skirt pushed up. I asked her to smack my ass, and she did, and clearly enjoyed it. But—explaining she felt too silly—she couldn't take the initiative to do it on her own. I eased her into it by asking for each smack before she delivered it and by the end of our playtime my obvious physical excitement was enough to make her want to spank me every time we had sex.

What kind of spanking is this going to be? Are two of you going to team up on the third person? Are you going to spank two asses at once, you lucky dog? Perhaps you will perform a spanking while the other person watches? Set up the scene before you begin.

Tips for Giving a Hot Spanking

1. FIND A SEX POSITION. Bent over something is always a crowd pleaser. Beds, couches, laps, all of these are good options.

2. WARM UP. Don't just start smacking away. Start with light taps. Rub his or her cute little butt in between smacks to keep the connection.

3. MAKE YOUR SPANKING RECIPIENT count the hits as you go. If you are really mean, you can make them thank you.

4. TALK A BLUE STREAK. You know how to talk dirty. Now do it. Tell your bottom what a bad boy he is. Tell him exactly what you plan to do to him.

5. CONCENTRATE your smacks on the fleshy part of the ass. This is safer, feels better, and sends a lot of nice reverb throughout the genitals.

6. ADD SOME EXTRAS. Hair pulling is nice. Try it out and see. Softly at first, you want to turn him or her on, not piss her off.

7. COMPLIMENT HIS OR HER ASS. Tell your spankee how nice they look bent over.

8. USE A PADDLE. I have bruised my hand on quite a few rumps. Don't let this happen to you.

9. COOL DOWN. When you get near the end of the spanking ask your naughty little bottom how they would like to cool down. They might want the taps to come more slowly, or maybe they want them more softly.

10. BASK IN THE AFTERGLOW. Hug, cuddle, fuck, or do whatever it is you like to do after intense sex play.

ROLE-PLAY

Role-playing games are extra fun for threeway participants, just think of the options. You've got more cast members to work with—meaning you can put on a more impressive show. Be clever. Act ridiculous. It's just sex.

Try pretending to be Bob Fosse and some slutty chorus girls. Or two of you can be mean prison guards dealing with a new inmate. You can pretend to be bad students and a strict teacher, or Swedish twins and a pornographer. My lover once woke me up on Easter morning and started an impromptu scene between Jesus and Mary Magdalene. Her benevolent eyes gazed lustfully at my tempting body and we had hot sex like only a messiah and a Roman hooker know how. It was way better than an egg hunt.

Role-play gives your sex life endless opportunities for new fun sexual scenarios. And it means you'll never get bored with your lovers since they can essentially become a new person whenever you want. Playing this way involves a little suspension of disbelief, but what part of sex doesn't? The best way to get into it is to keep your sense of humor. Relax and have fun and pick roles based on the sexual dynamic you are looking for. Don't agree to play slave boy if you aren't into a little cock and ball torture. And if what you really want is to get hog tied, then mean boss isn't the right role for you.

Be creative. Use props. Dress the part. I like to keep a box of costumes around for impromptu cop-and-robber scenes and trucker gang bangs because you just never know when you might want that kind of thing. Think of role-play as a Halloween party for your bedroom. You know how Halloween is just an excuse for the popular girls to dress like sluts? Well, role-playing games allow you to don bunny ears and fishnets whenever the mood strikes.

SOME GREAT ROLE PLAY IDEAS FOR THREEWAYS:

- Pirate captain and fair maidens
- Amazon warriors and captive
- Rebelling secretaries and frightened boss

- Firefighters and rescuees
- Cops and robbers
- Models and photographers
- Kidnappers and hostages
- Bank robbers and tellers
- Sluts and bikers
- Priests and choir boys
- Catholic girls and bad boys
- Sultan and harem girls
- Grocery boys and soccer mom
- Mrs. Robinson and the Graduate (or two graduates)
- Mechanics and motorists

SAFER SEX

OK. I don't mean to be Captain Bring Down, but we need to have the safer sex talk. Regardless of your relationship status, if you have multiple partners you need to know how to play safe. There are lots of STDs out there, and the more people you play with, the more exposure you have. And if you happen to be in a committed relationship, or a noncommitted relationship, or anything that involves other people, it's your responsibility to keep your partners as well as yourself safe and disease free. But fear not intrepid sex fiend! Latex barriers are your friends. Don't leave home without them.

Condoms

Use them, duh. I mean if you don't know you should use condoms by now you really don't deserve to have a threeway. Regular condom usage reduces the risk of HIV transmission by 10,000 times. And while condoms cannot protect you from every disease out there, they sure as hell help.

Use a condom on your penis. Switch the condom anytime you switch holes. This means from pussy to ass, or from wife's pussy to girlfriend's pussy, or wife's pussy to boyfriend's mouth. Anytime your penis goes into anything new, it needs to have a fresh condom on it.

Use a condom on your dildo. Switch the condom anytime you switch holes. While you aren't going to get an infection from your silicone buddy, you can drag bacteria and viruses from one partner to another. Switch the condom anytime your dildo goes into a new hole.

Use condoms on your sex toys. Anything insertable needs latex. Slip bullet vibrators into condoms, and switch the condom before you hand off the vibe. Slip a condom onto your butt plugs, this makes them easier to clean up. Put a condom on anything that goes inside you or anyone else present.

Don't whine about wearing a condom ever. And don't under any circumstances have sex with anyone who whines about wearing a condom. If one or both of your would-be threeway participants balk at using latex barriers, climb down from the kitchen table, pull up your G string, and go home.

Dental Dams

These little latex sheets are designed to be held over the genitals while dining at the Y, or held over the butt hole for germ-free rimming. They allow you to enjoy risk-free oral sex but arguably can be a pain to maneuver. However, I'm guessing that when you get it through your head that most STDs that live down South can also take up residence in your throat, you'll probably get friendly with dams.

Saran Wrap is a great alternative to dental dams. Wrap up your special friend in a little cling wrap and eat till you're full. Saran Wrap is great because you can tear off big sheets and lick from ass to pussy and back again with no risk of germ sharing. It also makes a very good impromptu bondage material.

Latex Gloves

Latex gloves have always been popular with the Sapphic set, and are also common for piercing scenes or anything else that might involve blood. The rest of the world really should get with the program and glove up. Latex gloves not only make your hands more slippery, meaning decreased friction burns, but they keep you from hurting your partner with sharp fingernails, or rough cuticles.

You should wear latex gloves if you are going to penetrate your partner with your fingers and change to a fresh glove before putting those fingers anywhere else. Wearing gloves allows you to penetrate someone anally and then vaginally without leaving the room to wash-up. Try wearing two gloves, and stripping one off before you switch partners or holes.

•••

There are an awful lot of things you can do with three of you. And this chapter hopefully gave you some ideas beyond plain ol' genital sex, not that I'm knocking it. We've covered a little kink, erotic massage, role-play, and rounded it all out with a lecture about latex. I think you're good to go. You don't have to buy a bunch of supplies, or sign any contracts. You can play around and figure out what you like. Hopefully this will all make your threeway more fun. In the next chapter we'll talk about the different positions that the three of you can get into.

CHAPTER 8

POSITIONS

WE'VE COVERED A LOT of ground by now. You know how to talk dirty, tie someone up, use toys, negotiate boundaries, find willing partners, and all that. But what about plain ol' intercourse? There are three of you, so making the beast with two backs won't work. Well, lucky for you I've come up with some tried-and-true positions for you to try out. Some of these were suggested by other threeway participants and some of these came out of threeways I've been in myself.

WHAT KINDS OF THINGS CAN THREE PEOPLE DO IN A BED?

Well three people can do anything two people can do, only with more hands, mouths, cocks, and pussies. The beauty of threeways is the many options they afford you. You can fuck or get fucked while watching someone masturbate. You can lie back and eat bonbons while your wife does it with the cable guy. You are only limited by your imagination.

OK, Casanova, it's just sex, right? Nothing to worry about, you're a pro by now. You've probably done it a million times. You've read the chapters on processing and negotiating. You've attended a few orgies. And you're ready to try out all your new skills. No, you don't need a blueprint for your threeway. You'll have plenty of fun just figuring it out along the way. But trust me, with all those extra arms and legs in the bed things *can* get a little confusing. As long as everyone communicates and pays close attention to the other two bodies there's no reason why your threesome should be anything besides a totally over-the-top orgasmic experience.

> *I play regularly with two other guys. We all get together once in a while and have sex. They are a couple, but they date other people. I like the relationship I have with them because I primarily feel like we are good friends. Anyway, one night I was fucking one of them while his boyfriend watched and jerked off. I had the guy on his back with his legs in the air and I was pounding him really hard. Eventually I flipped him over so that he was on his hands and knees and his boyfriend got closer so we could make out while he jerked off. I found myself totally fixated on watching him jerk off. It was almost as if he was jerking off my cock as well as his own. That was a hot night.*
>
> —T, 31

Positions

Here are a few positions to try out and some tales from a few real-life threeway enthusiasts to get you in the mood. It's good to augment any of these positions with toys, or blindfolds, or video cameras, or anything else that gets you excited. Just consider the following positions as suggestions and go from there. A little inspiration never hurt anyone.

THE DAISY CHAIN

This position is a classic—and very popular with gay men. But the beauty of it is that it is adaptable for any combo of genders using any combo of poles and holes. Essentially it consists of three people connected to each other by penetrating or being penetrated by one of the other parties. The person in the middle wins the extra special prize of doing and getting done both at the same time.

STOCKHOLM SYNDROME

One of you is restrained, preferably to a chair, while the other two get down with each other in every way possible. The restrained party gets to watch all the action but doesn't get to touch. If you really, really love him or her, you can untie him or her at the end and let them join the party.

NO HOLES BARRED

This is a double-penetration position and works best with at least one female present since, of course, girls have two holes and boys only have one. Although over-achieving anal sex enthusiasts can certainly try and take more than one tool in their special place at a time if they are so inclined. I mean, far be it for me to set limits.

One person lies down on his or her back while the lucky soon-to-be-filled lady climbs aboard the cock or strap-on, whichever it happens to be. She then leans forward so that the third person can penetrate her ass from behind. This takes a little practice but it sure is worth it.

MUSTACHE RIDES

This is an all-oral extravaganza and works well for any combination of genders and bodies. Think Daisy Chain, only everyone is going South. One lucky licker lies down, while another one of you climbs on his or her face. The third person lies down between his or her legs and performs oral sex to their little heart's content.

THE DAGWOOD

So-called because you are stacked up like a sandwich. Two of you lie on top of each other, either on your back or stomach, or maybe even one of each. The third party penetrates one and then the other of you with his or her cock, strap-on, or fingers, alternating between bodies.

THE CIRCLE JERK

It's a party and everyone's coming! Never underestimate the hot factor of mutual masturbation, and with three of you it's even hotter. Everyone lies around in a circle, or stands around, or sits, or some combination of the three. Just make sure you have a clear picture of everyone involved. And you all jerk off in whatever manner you enjoy. Put on a good show, the hot part of this position is getting to watch and be watched at the same time.

THE TRIANGLE

One of you lies on his or her back while the other two climb aboard face and cock respectively. This works well for three ladies if the bottom person is wearing a strap-on or if you angle it just right for a little muff-to-muff action. The two people on top can lean forward and make out with each other, thus forming the two sides of the triangle.

ON THE BENCH

OK, it's a dumb name, but it does require a bench of some sort for best results. You could probably work it out with an ottoman, or foot stool, but a weight bench, or piano bench works very well. One of you lies on the bench on your back, knees up. This leaves your ass free for rimming, fucking, or anything else you like to do with an ass. And remember what we learned in the anatomy chapter? The ass is a gender-free hole, everyone has one! While you are being rimmed or fucked, the other person stands over your face and masturbates while talking dirty about how they are going to come all over you.

THE PORCUPINE

So called because it has a couple of pricks. This requires a thigh harness, available at most sex toy stores. This works well for any combo of genders and bodies. One person lies on their back while another leans over them and sucks his or her cock or strap-on. The other person mounts a second strap-on attached to person number one's thigh. This isn't the easiest combo to manage, but with a little maneuvering, it's pretty rewarding. Ever wished you had more than one cock? Well, now you do! You get to penetrate two people at once, you lucky bastard.

THE GROUP GROPE

Everyone lies down on their backs and caresses the person next to them. It doesn't matter which part you get your hands on; the point is for everyone to be touching or being touched at the same time. The point with this position is to build up the group energy. Don't take your hands away or break the energy cycle until at least one of you climaxes.

Remember, these are just suggestions. Any combo of parts in a bed is going to be fun. Use your imagination, get creative. Play with top and bottom roles, bring in power play, order your partners around, or beg them to fuck you. And most importantly relax and enjoy yourself.

●●●

> *I think my favorite thing to do in a threeway is to get double penetrated. You can do that with just one person, but with two it's more exciting. The last time I did this I was having a threeway with my best friend and her husband and one of them penetrated my vagina with fingers and one penetrated my ass with a toy. It was amazing. It's a totally overwhelming sensation.*
>
> — D, 32

My girlfriend and I started having sex really loudly one night while my roommate, Robin, was home. We had both wanted to have sex with her for a while but didn't know how to make it happen spontaneously. We were being really loud on purpose to see if she'd come in and join us, but I guess she was too shy. Finally my girlfriend got the idea to go to her room and ask if we could borrow her lube. That apparently got the idea across because she came to her door in just boxers and she and my girlfriend started making out right there. Finally the two of them came into my room and my girlfriend pushed Robin onto the bed and I held her arms above her head while my girlfriend pulled down her jeans and started playing with her pussy through her boxers. Robin started begging to get fucked and I held her arms down and talked dirty to her while my girlfriend fisted her.

—S, 26

One New Year's Eve I stayed late at a party after everyone else had gone home. The party was hosted by a couple I'd always had a little flirtation with—but I never really imagined I'd follow through with anything. Anyway, we'd all been drinking champagne and I was feeling turned on and sexy. The host put on some music and his wife and I began dancing with each other.

She was gorgeous, very short and curvy with large breasts. I'm very athletic with no boobs; I never even wear a bra because I'm so flat chested. I remember finding myself getting really excited by the differences in our bodies. She had this long black hair that hung down to the middle of her back, and olive skin, and big brown almond shaped eyes. I scooped up her hair and used it as leverage to pull her head back and kiss her. We stayed like that forever, just slowly swaying to the music and kissing. I don't know what her husband was doing at that point. Probably just enjoying the show. I finally realized I wasn't all that interested in doing anything sexual with him, but I really wanted to make love to her.

I stripped off her tank top and ran my hands over her lacy bra. We made out some more until finally she suggested we go into the bedroom. I stripped her naked and laid her down on the bed and began licking her pussy. She was dripping wet and moaning and begging me to stick my fingers inside her. I finally entered her really roughly with three fingers and began to fuck her very hard. She was very excited and was kind of bucking against my arm. She was so wet and turned on that I slipped another finger in and she started rubbing her clit until she screamed loudly and ejaculated all over my arm. We didn't say anything. We just crawled under the sheets and curled up next to each other and fell asleep.

Her husband was just watched everything, he never even came near us. I can't even remember if he jerked off or not. I just have this image of him remaining politely at a distance while I fucked his wife.

—K, 34

VOYEURISM AND EXHIBITIONISM

Do you like to watch or be watched? One of the neat pluses to multiple-partner sex is the chance to see people having real sex right in front of you or to have sex while someone watches. A threeway affords you the perfect opportunity to indulge an exhibitionist or voyeuristic fantasy. You and another participant can perform for a third person, or you can lie back and watch while the other two go at it like bunnies. Some of my favorite threeways have involved watching my lover with another person, or having another person watch me get fucked.

A voyeur is someone who gets turned on by watching. Going to strip clubs and peep shows and watching porn are forms of voyeurism. So is watching your lover masturbate or watching two of your lovers have sex during a threeway. An exhibitionist gets turned on while being watched or looked at in a sexual way. Dressing up in slutty lingerie for your lover, performing strip teases, masturbating for your lover, and performing sexually with another person while your lover watches are all forms of exhibitionism.

My old apartment complex had a kind of *Rear Window* effect to it: you could see what was going on in apartments across the way just like in the Hitchcock film. San Francisco is a sexed-up city and it often seemed like the neighbors were putting on shows for each other all the time. I remember seeing people in other apartments masturbate all the time, and we had so many windows in our apartment that I just sort of assumed people could see me having sex with my partner during the day.

I lived in that place back in my days as the editor of *On Our Backs* magazine and we often did porn shoots in one of the rooms. My favorite shoot involved a gorgeous woman who happened to be seven months pregnant, wearing nothing but eight inch platforms. I'm sure the neighborhood voyeurs were happy that day.

A friend was once indulging his voyeuristic side in that old apartment by watching two women who were slow dancing naked in front of their living room window. He turned out his bedroom lights and assuming no one could see him, started jerking off with the two naked girls as fodder.

The girls indulged their exhibitionist tendencies by putting on a sexy show with each other in front of their window and he indulged his voyeuristic tendencies by watching them. Then as he was getting close to climaxing he looked around and realized that across the way, in the same building as the naked girls, there was a man standing naked in front of the window watching him, and stroking a raging hard-on. My friend was too far gone to care and masturbated while watching the naked girls and the guy watched him. So in effect, it was a nice little threeway and my friend was both voyeur and exhibitionist.

Watching people have sex is incredibly intimate and arousing, and it's something we don't often get to experience. Even in multiple-partner sex situations we may not feel comfortable hanging back and watching the action for fear of being judged or thought of as weird. But our voyeuristic sides get teased constantly by everything around us. Sex is used to sell everything from cars to toothpaste. Going full throttle and watching real sex take place in front of our eyes is much more satisfying than getting constantly cock-teased by MTV.

Greta Christina, author of *Paying for It: A Guide by Sex Workers for Their Clients*, points out that events as seemingly innocuous as going to a strip club and watching your boyfriend or girlfriend get a lap dance or even just putting money into a strippers G string is a way of engaging voyeuristically in a threeway, and couples who are interested in inviting someone into their sex play can start by playing with strippers and other sex performers.

> *I love going to strip clubs with my butch girlfriend and watching her get lap dances. It really turns me on to watch her and watch the stripper getting off on each other. Every club we've been to it seemed like the girls were really into having female clients and I always sense a certain amount of excitement on the dancers' parts as well as my girlfriend's.*
>
> —C, 42

•••

I was at a bar with a large group of friends and one of the girls that was in our party turned out to be a stripper. My girlfriend decided she wanted to watch me have a lap dance. so she asked the girl if she'd give me one and she readily agreed. I wasn't all that into it. I did it more for my girlfriend. She, on the other hand, really seemed to get into it.

—G, 32

Porn director and videographer Sydney Masters has had many opportunities to watch people have sex. "It's different when you know what goes on behind the scenes," says Masters. "Most porn is contrived, and the actors are really performing for the camera. Not that they aren't enjoying themselves, but what most of us get to see when we watch porn is consciously acted out. It's the between-takes moments between the actors that I have always found the most interesting."

Masters, who has worked with some of the biggest names in the business, as well as shot small independent queer videos and played regularly in various SM scenes says that one of the things that struck her about watching porn stars perform surprised her. "It was the sound of people having real sex that I found mesmerizing. The way they breathe and the sounds they make when they have a real orgasm, that really struck me. I worked with Janine [Lindenmuller] and she was just amazing. She's a very experimental actress and she really gets into what she's doing. I remember being fascinated by the noises she'd make. Watching authentic sex is a very moving experience."

Masters explains that one of the roles she's enjoyed playing is that of helper during intense SM scenes. "I like to make sure that whoever is playing has everything they need. I like to provide toys, wipe sweat from faces, bring water, and just generally be involved as a facilitator and supportive presence." It's very satisfying to play this role during a threeway as well.

Try lying back and watching your two partners get it on. Notice the things they do, make note of the way they stimulate themselves and each other. If you are watching your primary partner with someone else, then this is your chance to see how they get turned on and get off. Pay close attention and learn from the experience. Michael Smith, the CEO of Tantus Silicone, says "Watching your lover with someone else is a very selfless experience. It's your one chance to concentrate fully on your partner's pleasure and to notice what he or she does when they aren't conscious of it. It's a very intimate and loving part of a threeway."

Your exhibitionist fantasies can also come out during a threeway. Perhaps you've had fantasies of being watched while having sex? Maybe even by your lover? A threeway is a good time to indulge yourself. Budding exhibitionists may want to read Carol Queen's *Exhibitionism for the Shy: Show Off, Dress Up and Talk Hot*. The book details her transformation from shy wallflower to a woman fully in charge of her sexuality.

You can indulge your exhibitionist fantasies during a threeway by masturbating while the other two participants watch. You can fuck one person while the other watches. You can instruct one person not to move, maybe forbid them to touch you, and then perform oral sex on them. You can give lap dances, dress sexy, and be aware of your body and movements. There are many ways to show off your sex appeal during sex but a threeway makes it even more exciting because there are more eyes to watch you. If you are a single person and you are having sex with a couple, then a threeway is really your perfect stage. Think of the couple as your audience and put all of your energy into being a sex machine. Get off on yourself. You are the special guest star in their relationship and that is a very powerful and sexy position.

I like wearing short skirts around my girlfriend. She always tries to push my skirt up or put her hand under it when we are in public. She has a very high sex drive, which I love. I try to encourage it whenever possible. Lately she's been fantasizing about having a threeway, though we haven't done it yet. Her fantasy is to watch me get fucked by someone else while she facilitates in some way either by holding my legs apart or pushing my dress up. I really get off on this idea and want to make it happen but we haven't found the right person yet. I like the idea of her watching me while I get fucked very hard. I want her to be so turned on that she can't help but jerk off while she watches. Sometimes she fantasies about me being over her lap while another woman fucks me with her strap-on and sometimes I'm bent over the bed or somewhere else in the room and she's hanging back watching me. I get really turned on when she stares at me. Even when I'm fully dressed I get horny from her looking at me and thinking about sex. I think I would be very turned on if she watched me get fucked by someone else.

—K, 27

Now that we've covered some of the things that three bodies can do in a bed it's time to move on and talk about the morning after. What happens when it's over? How do you say good-bye after a night of hot sex, or a morning of postcoital brunch. And what if your threeway turns into a long-term thing? Threeway relationships can be very rewarding, but also challenging. In the next chapter we'll talk about how to leave on a high note, or stick around if that's what everyone wants.

CHAPTER 9

THE MORNING AFTER

MOST OF WHAT I'VE covered in this book has to do with sex between three people, but not necessarily the interpersonal relations or feelings that go hand in hand with threeways of all formations. In this chapter we'll talk a little bit about emotional aftercare and what to do if you find your threeway fling has turned into a relationship.

How's Your Head?

One of the things I hope you've taken away from this book is that you should treat everyone you climb in bed with—regardless of your preexisting relationship—with respect. Be upfront about your desires. Communicate honestly and leave your issues at home, or at least have the decency to work through them quietly if you must bring them to bed with you.

So what happens when everyone's spent and it's time to go home? Do you simply sling your panties over your shoulder and bid the players adieu? How does everyone feel? You may need to check in and debrief a bit before you do the walk of shame in last night's party outfit.

ENDING GRACEFULLY

No matter what your arrangement you should end your sexy fun with grace and respect for everyone involved. If you've made arrangements before the fun started about who sleeps where or who goes home and who stays, then stick with the plan. It's OK to change it if you need to, but make sure everyone is in agreement before inviting your guest to sleep over or deciding you need to leave. He or she may really want to sleep in his or her own bed; sometimes intimacy and sex are two separate entities.

Show affection to your playmates. Don't shut down after you get your rocks off. Even if you've had a long hard night of sweaty sex and you're all three exhausted checking out is bad manners. If someone is leaving, make sure they have transportation or cab fare. Say your good-byes. If you had a great time, say so. If everyone is staying, make sure you each have a place to sleep. You may or may not want to make plans to see each other again. It's OK either way. No one should feel pressured. Make sure you all have ways to contact each other. Be honest with yourself and your new playmates. If this was a one-time thing, don't say you will call. If you want another go, say so and agree to talk in a few days to set up a date.

For Couples

Take care of each other and take care of your special guest. Remember that the two of you have each other forever. You may want to put your relationship on hold and spend some time reassuring your guest how much fun your time together was. If he or she spent the night, then coffee and small talk in bed is definitely a better option than an uncomfortable exit with mumbled good-byes. Make your new lover feel special and adored. As much as casual sex and occasional hook ups can be very enjoyable experiences, there's still a bond that gets created when you are sexually intimate with someone. Respect that emotional bond. It doesn't mean you have to fall in love. But acknowledging that you've spent some very special time together is important. Never make a person you've had sex with feel uncomfortable in your bed. Allow him or her, as well as yourself and your partner, enough time to come down from your erotic high and leave on a positive note.

Leaving Alone

If you were hooked up with a couple or two others you'd just met, you'll probably be leaving alone. How do you feel? If it's exactly the way you wanted it to be, that's wonderful. I hope your threeway experience was a great one and you are skipping home in your dancing shoes with a postcoital spring in your step.

Don't make a mad exit from anyone's bed. Stick around until everyone's awake. Spend time together in the morning. Talk about the night before. If it was everything you dreamed it would be, say so. Tell the couple how much you enjoyed yourself, and then make your exit allowing them some time to reconnect as a twosome. If you were with two people you just met, spend a little time hanging out. Exchange numbers or make plans to see each other again if you like. If you prefer not to hook up again, that's OK too. It's important for everyone to respect the desires of everyone else. Keep egos in check.

Even if things went differently than planned, there's no reason to run screaming from the room. If you are eager to leave because you feel uncomfortable for some reason then explain to your bedmates that you've got to go home and feed the cat or dog or roommate or whatever. Make a polite exit.

WHEN NO ONE WANTS TO LEAVE

Sometimes you start out an evening thinking you are about to have a fun little romp with no strings attached, but you wake up between two bodies and realize that no one wants to go home. Or maybe you play with each other enough times that it's no longer just casual sex. Suddenly your threeway looks a little different. It looks like a relationship. Yikes, what do you do now?

So what happens if all this slutting around and having threeways leads to falling in love? The straight coupled-up, totally monogamous, till-death-do-you-part marriage is the only thing sanctioned by society, religion, the law, your parents, you name it. Many of us are so socialized to believe in monogamy and marriage that we can't even imagine something that doesn't look like it. It's OK to think about sex in all sorts of alternative forms, but sex is something we tend to keep private. You don't have to bring your sex partners home to Mom. But what happens when you get involved with them?

Some of the guys and gals who answered my survey mentioned that ongoing triads were probably their favorite types of relationship and that the benefits of being in an ongoing threeway shouldn't be overlooked. For one thing, there are three of you to take care of each other. If one partner is busy with things outside the relationship, things like work, family, friends, and other regular life issues, there are two other people available to form a supportive net. A combination of genders and sexual orientations can offer a balance of perspectives that you might not get from a couple relationship. And with three of you, there's more love and affection to go around.

The problems of a triad are pretty much the same as the problems in any other relationship. Partners need to communicate enough to avoid things like jealousy, insecurity, and misunderstandings. All involved parties will have different emotional and physical needs. They will all require different levels of intimacy as well as different amounts of attention and time alone. Oftentimes one third of a trio will want sex less or more often than the other two. Or everyone will want it at different times. It's hard enough to line up the sex drives of two people, but add a third and it gets really messy.

You Don't Have to Live Together

Just because you are in a threeway relationship doesn't mean you need to all shack up together. You might discover that even though you love the sex, and you love hanging out together, your lifestyles and the way you view money, privacy, housing, and all the other long term relationship stuff are way too different to work as housemates. That's OK. Your relationship model is an alternative one, and there's no reason your living situation shouldn't be, too. You can still have a loving committed relationship in a way that works for you even if you keep three separate apartments.

Some things to keep in mind in an ongoing threeway relationship:

Be Sensitive to Any Type of Primary/Secondary Relationship Issues

There's probably a history to your threeway relationship. Chances are you didn't all three meet simultaneously. If two people were a couple before you got started, they know each other better, they possibly have their own set of preexisting issues and a deeper understanding of each other. A couple may have to work extra hard to ensure that the new person feels like an equal member of the triad.

The New Addition

As the new person it's your duty to understand that a long-term couple is going to know each other very well and have a lot of history together. This shouldn't keep you from feeling like an equal partner. Regardless of how much love and heat are present at the beginning of a threeway relationship, you'll probably feel less connected because you've had less time in the relationship. When you first start out this is a sort of safety valve. You've got less invested and can leave if you feel like it isn't working out. But if things progress, an intimacy imbalance can make things a little weird. Make sure to air your fears as they come up. And it's helpful to spend some alone time with each half of the couple in order to establish a bond with each of them individually.

For All Three of You

Try to keep from having secrets between any two partners. Work on maintaining an air of openness and honesty. There are three of you and if two people have secrets or issues that they haven't aired to the other one, it's bound to lead to trouble. It's important that no one feels alienated. Encourage couple behavior as well as alone time. Break off into twos from time to time and do some pair bonding. Allow each member of the threesome to have their own individuality and identity. Keep in mind that three people aren't going to fall in love, take risks, and alter their lives all at the same rate. Everyone's rate of change is different.

•••

Hopefully your threeway relationship will be a happy one full of lots of love and passion and sex. The guidelines I've laid out above are just a start. You should read anything you can get your hands on about polyamory and alternative relationships. Check the resource guide for suggestions about books and support groups. Seek out other poly types and make friends with folks who get your unique relationship. You'll need support and understanding and experienced people who've been there can help you get through the rough spots and help you celebrate the great parts.

•••

So long! Farewell!

Well kids, here we are at the end. Just like Mr. Rogers says, I'm so glad we had this time together. If there's anything I like talking about it's sex, and I've done just that for almost 200 pages. I sure hope you've enjoyed yourself as much as I have. If this book encourages you to take off into the land of threeway adventures, then my work here is done. Just remember that beyond books, toys, porn, lube, Belladonna, race cars, dog collars, dildos, and all the other ingredients in a great sex life, the most important parts of the recipe will always be an open mind, good communication skills, and a desire to learn. Check out the resources section for places to learn more about sex from every angle you can think of. I wish you a lifetime of good sex.

Now go outside and play.

ACKNOWLEDGMENTS

THIS BOOK WOULD NEVER have gotten off the ground without a lot of help from a bunch of people in my life. Thanks to Angela Brown for pitching me the idea and thanks to Shannon Berning for being a patient and encouraging editor. I'd also like to thank Christophe, Heather, Rebekah, and the entire staff at Blowfish for the wonderful sex ed discussions we've had as part of our *Radio Blowfish Variety Show*. I've learned a lot working with them and they've been a great source of information.

Thanks to Ian Hendrie for starting out with me, and sticking with me through all of it. Thanks to Lu Read for rounding up threeways and sharing stories with me, and Irena for all the work dates and sex talk. And I'd especially like to thank everyone who responded to all my personal questions about their sex lives. Your honesty is completely appreciated.

RESOURCE GUIDE

Read books, watch porn, surf the Web. The more you know about sex, the better lover you will be.

BOOKS

General Sex Ed Books

Dr. Sprinkle's Spectacular Sex, by Annie Sprinkle
Exhibitionism for the Shy, by Carol Queen
The Good Vibrations Guide to Sex, by Cathy Winks and Anne Semans
Guide to Getting It On!, by Paul Joannides
Down and Dirty Sex Secrets, by Tristan Taormino
The Big Bang: Nerve's Guide to the New Sexual Universe, by the writers at *Nerve*
The Hot Guide to Safer Sex, by Yvonne K. Fulbright
The Complete Idiot's Guide to Amazing Sex, by Sari Locker
Orgasms for Two: The Joy of Partnersex, by Betty Dodson
Sex for the Clueless: How to Enjoy a More Erotic and Exciting Life, by Marcy Sheiner
The KISS Guide to Sex, by Anne Hooper

Books Specifically About Having Sex with Women

She Comes First: The Thinking Man's Guide to Pleasuring a Woman, by Ian Kerner
Lesbian Sex Secrets for Men, Amy Goddard, by Kurt Brungardt

On Our Backs *Guide to Lesbian Sex*, by Diana Cage
The Lesbian Sex Book, by Wendy Caster and Rachel Kramer Bussel
The Whole Lesbian Sex Book, by Felice Newman
The Straight Girl's Guide to Sleeping with Chicks, by Jen Sincero
Female Ejaculation and the G-Spot, by Deborah Sundahl
The Good Vibrations Guide: The G-Spot, by Cathy Winks
The Good Orgasm Guide: All a Girl Needs for a Great Time, by Kate Taylor
Expanded Orgasm, by Patricia Taylor
Tricks . . . to Please a Woman, by Jay Wiseman

Having Sex with Men

Sex Tips for Straight Women from a Gay Man, by Dan Anderson and Maggie Berman
Tricks . . . to Please a Man, by Jay Wiseman
Gay Sex: A Manual for Men Who Love Men, by Jack Hart
101 Gay Sex Secrets Revealed, by Jonathon Bass

Masturbation for Gals

Sex for One: The Joy of Selfloving, by Betty Dodson
Good Vibrations: The New Complete Guide to Vibrators, by Joani Blank, Ann Whidden
Tickle Your Fancy: A Woman's Guide to Sexual Self-Pleasure, by Sadie Allison

Multiple Os

ESO: How You and Your Lover Can Give Each Other Hours of Extended Sexual Orgasm, by Donna Brauer
The Multi-Orgasmic Man: Sexual Secrets Every Man Should Know, by Mantak Chia and Douglas Abrams Arava
The Multi-Orgasmic Couple, by Mantak Chia
Male Multiple Orgasm Step by Step, by Jack Johnston

Oral Sex

The Ultimate Guide to Cunnilingus, by Violet Blue
The Low Down on Going Down: How to Give Her Mind-Blowing Oral Sex, by Marcy Michaels, Marie Des
Box Lunch: The Layperson's Guide to Cunnilingus, by Diana Cage
The Ultimate Guide to Fellatio, by Violet Blue
Blow Him Away: How to Give Him Mind-Blowing Oral Sex, by Marcy Michaels, Marie Des
Going Down: The Instinct Guide to Oral Sex, by Ben R. Rogers

Erotic Massage

Sensual Massage for Couples, by Gordon Inkeles

Anal Sex

The Ultimate Guide to Anal Sex for Men, by Bill Brent
The Ultimate Guide to Anal Sex for Women, by Tristan Taormino
Anal Pleasure and Health: A Guide for Men and Women, by Jack Morin

Dirty Talk

Exhibitionism for the Shy, by Carol Queen
Phone Sex: Aural Thrills and Oral Skills, by Miranda Austin
Sex Talk: Uncensored Exercises for Exploring What Really Turns You On, by Aline P. Zoldbrod, Ph.D., and Lauren Dockett
The Fine Art of Erotic Talk: How to Entice, Excite, and Enchant Your Lover with Words, by Bonnie Gabriel
Talk Sexy to the One You Love, by Barbara Keesling

Sex Toys

Sex Toys 101: A Playfully Uninhibited Guide, by Rachel Venning and Claire Cavanah
The Ultimate Guide to Strap-On Sex, by Karlyn Lotney
The Toybag Guide to High-Tech Toys, by John Warren

The Many Joys of Sex Toys: The Ultimate How-to Handbook for Couples and Singles, by Anne Semans

BDSM

Sensuous Magic: A Guide to S/M for Adventurous Couples, by Patrick Califia

Screw the Roses, Send Me the Thorns: The Romance and Sexual Sorcery of Sadomasochism, by Phillip Miller and Molly Devon

The New Bottoming Book / The New Topping Book, by Dossie Easton and Janet Hardy

Consensual Sadomasochism: How to Talk About It and How to Do It Safely, by Bill Henkin and Sybil Holiday

SM 101: A Realistic Introduction, by Jay Wiseman

Safe, Sane, Consensual and Fun, by John Warren

Role-playing

The Ultimate Guide to Sexual Fantasy: How to Turn Your Fantasies into Reality, by Violet Blue

Fantasy Made Flesh: The Essential Guide to Erotic Roleplay, by Deborah Addington

Various Fun Activities

Consensual Spanking, by Jules Markham

Erotic Tickling, by Michael Moran

Flogging, by Joseph Bean

Erotic Bondage Handbook, by Jay Wiseman

The Seductive Art of Japanese Bondage, by Midori

The Mistress Manual: The Good Girl's Guide to Female Dominance, by Lorelei

Training with Miss Abernathy: A Workbook for Erotic Slaves and Their Owners, by Christina Abernathy

Miss Abernathy's Concise Slave Training Manual, by Christina Abernathy

SlaveCraft: Roadmaps for Erotic Servitude, by Guy Baldwin
The Toybag Guide to Canes and Caning, Janet Hardy
The Toybag Guide to Foot and Shoe Worship, by Midori
The Toybag Guide to Clips and Clamps, by Jack Rinella
The Toybag Guide to Hot Wax and Temperature Play, by Sectrum
The Toybag Guide to Erotic Knife Play, by Miranda Austin
The Toybag Guide to Dungeon Emergencies and Supplies, by Jay Wiseman
Family Jewels: A Guide to Male Genital Play and Torment, by Midori

Alternative Dating and Relationships

The Kinky Girl's Guide to Dating, by Luna Gray
Partners in Power: Living in Kinky Relationships, by Jack Rinella
Radical Ecstasy, by Dossie Easton and Catherine A. Liszt
The Ethical Slut, by Dossie Easton and Catherine A. Liszt
Coming Out: When Someone You Love Is Kinky, by Dossie Easton and Catherine A. Liszt
Painfully Obvious, by Robert Davolt

Fisting

A Hand in the Bush: The Fine Art of Vaginal Fisting, by Deborah Addington
Trust, the Hand Book: A Guide to the Sensual and Spiritual Art of Handballing, by Bert Herrman

Good Smut

Best American Erotica series, ed. by Susie Bright
Best Lesbian Erotica series, ed. by Tristan Taormino
Best Transgender Erotica, ed. by Hanne Blank and Raven Kaldera
Doing It for Daddy: Short Sexy Fiction About a Very Forbidden Fantasy, ed. by Pat Califia
Herotica Series, Vol. 1–7, ed. by various editors
The Leather Daddy and the Femme, by Carol Queen

Leatherwomen III: The Clash of the Cultures, ed. by Laura Antoniou
Macho Sluts, by Pat Califia
Melting Point, by Pat Califia
On Our Backs: The Best Erotic Fiction 1 and 2, ed. by Diana Cage
Speaking in Whispers: Lesbian African-American Erotica, by Kathleen E. Morris
Virgin Territory and Virgin Territory 2, ed. by Shar Rednour

VIDEOS AND DVDS

How to Be a Better Lover

Nina Hartley's Guide to Making Love to Women (Adam & Eve Productions, 2000)
Nina Hartley's Guide to Making Love to Men (Adam & Eve Productions, 2000)

Talk Dirty

Talk to Me Baby: A Lover's Guide to Dirty Talk and Role Play (S.I.R. Productions, 2004)

Dirty Dancing

Nina Hartley's Guide to Private Dancing (for men and women) (Adam & Eve Productions, 1997)

Oral Sex

Nina Hartley's Guide to Better Cunnilingus (Adam & Eve Productions, 1995)
Nina Hartley's Guide to Better Fellatio (Adam & Eve Productions, 1995)
Nina Hartley's Advanced Guide to Oral Sex (Adam & Eve Productions, 1995)
Better Oral Sex Techniques (Sinclair Intimacy Institute, 1997)

The G Spot

G Marks the Spot (Sex Positive Productions, 2003)
How to Female Ejaculate
How to Female Ejaculate; Find Your G-spot (Fatale Media, 1992)

Sexual Positions

The Complete Guide to Sexual Positions (Pacific Media Entertainment, 2002)
The Guide to Advanced Sexual Positions (Sinclair Intimacy Institue, 1995)
Creative Positions for Lovers (Sinclair Intimacy Institue, 1999)

Masturbation

Great Vibrations, by Carol Queen (Fatale Media, 1995)
Celebrating Orgasm, by Betty Dodson (Betty Dodson, 1996)
Solo Male Ecstasy: An Intimate Guide to Self-Pleasure (Pacific Media Entertainment, 1996)
Orgasmic Women: 13 Self-Loving Divas (Betty Dodson, 1996)

Sensual Massage

The Joy of Erotic Massage (Sinclair Intimacy Institute, 2001)
The Best of Vulva Massage (Erospirit Research Institute, 2000)

Butt Play

Nina Hartley's Guide to Anal Sex (Adam & Eve Productions, 1996)
Anal Massage for Lovers (Erospirit Research Institute, 2005)
Tristan Taormino's Ultimate Guide to Anal Sex for Women 1 and 2 (Evil Angel, 1999, 2001)
Tristan Taormino's House of Ass (Erospirit Research Institute, 2006)

Strap-Ons

Bend Over Boyfriend

Sex Toys

Nina Hartley's Guide to Sex Toys (Adam & Eve Productions, 1998)
Nina Hartley's Advanced Guide to Sex Toys (Adam & Eve Productions, 1999)
Toys for Better Sex (Sinclair Intimacy Institute, 2002)

Kink and BDSM

Whipsmart (Sex Positive Productions, 2001)
Fetish FAQ 1: Bondage (Bizarre Video, 2001)
Fetish FAQ 2: Nipple Play (Bizarre Video, 2000)
Fetish FAQ 3: Spanking (Bizarre Video, 2000)
Fetish FAQ 4: Playing Below the Belt (Bizarre Video, 2000)
The Pain Game: *Tie Me Up!* (Cleo Dubois, 2000)

Swinging

Nina Hartley's Guide to Swinging

Lesbian Porn

Afterschool Special/Turn Me Up Over & On (Fatale Media, 2005)
The Black Glove / The Elegant Spanking (Blue Productions, 2003)
The Boiler Room (Bleu Productions, 1998)
The Crash Pad (Blowfish Video, Inc. 2006)
Ecstasy in Berlin, 1926 (Bleu Productions, 2005)
Full Load (Fatale Media, 2002)
Hard Love & How to Fuck in High Heels (S.I.R. Video, 2000)
Ladies of the Night (Les Vampyres) / Let the Punishment Fit the Child (Bleu Productions, 2004)
The Seven Deadly Sins (Bleu Productions, 2005)
Silken Sleeves (Bleu Productions, 2006)
Sugar High Glitter City (S.I.R. Video, 2001)
Leda and the Swan—Nailed (Bleu Visions, 1999)
Voluptuous Vixens (Good Vibrations Sex Positive Productions, 2002)
Suburban Dykes (Fatale Video, 1990)

Bisexual Porn

Slide Bi Me (Good Vibrations' Sex Positive Productions, 2001)

Sex Info on the Web

SOCIETY FOR HUMAN SEXUALITY
www.sexuality.org

THE CLITORIS
www.the-clitoris.com

SEXUALITY INFORMATION & EDUCATION COUNCIL OF THE UNITED STATES
www.siecus.org

GO ASK ALICE!
www.goaskalice.columbia.edu

COALITION FOR POSITIVE SEXUALITY
www.positive.org

THE SOCIETY FOR THE ADVANCEMENT OF SEXUAL HEALTH
www.ncsac.org

HUMAN SEXUALITY, INC.
www.howtohavegoodsex.com

HOTLINES

AMERICAN SOCIAL HEALTH ASSOCIATION
(800) 971-8500

CENTERS FOR DISEASE CONTROL NATIONAL AIDS HOTLINE
(800) 342-AIDS
Spanish (800) 344-7432
Hearing impaired (800) 243-7889
www.cdcnac.com

DOMESTIC VIOLENCE HOTLINE
(800) 799-SAFE

HIV/AIDS TEEN HOTLINE
(800) 440-TEEN

LOS ANGELES SEX EDUCATION RESOURCES
(213) 486-4421

NATIONAL HERPES HOTLINE
(919) 361-8488

NATIONAL STD HOTLINE
(800) 227-8922

PLANNED PARENTHOOD
(800) 230-PLAN
www.ppfa.org

RAINN (RAPE ABUSE AND INCEST NATIONAL NETWORK)
(800) 656-HOPE

SAN FRANCISCO SEX INFORMATION
(877) 472-7374 toll-free
(415) 989-7374
www.sfsi.org

SEATTLE SEX INFORMATION
(206) 328-7711

PLACES TO SHOP FOR SEX STUFF

BLOWFISH
800-325-2569
www.blowfish.com

COME AS YOU ARE
701 Queen St. W.
Toronto, ON,
Canada M6J 1E6
(416) 504-7934
www.comeasyouare.com

CONDOMANIA
647 N. Poinsettia Place
Los Angeles, CA 90036
(323) 930-5530
(800) 926- 6366
351 Bleeker St.
New York, NY 10014
(212) 691-9442
www.condomania.com

CRIMSON PHOENIX
1876 SW 5th Ave.
Portland, OR 07201
(503) 228-0129

CUPID'S TREASURE
3519 N. Halstead
Chicago, IL 60657
(773) 348-3884

DREAM DRESSER
8444-50 Santa Monica Blvd.
West Hollywood, CA 90069
(800) 963-7326
1042 Wisconsin Ave, NW
Washington, D.C. 20007
(202) 625-0373
www.dreamdresser.com

EROS BOUTIQUE
581A Tremont St.
Boston, MA 02118
www.erosboutique.com

EVE'S GARDEN
119 W. 57th St.
Ste. #420
New York, NY 10019
(800) 848-3837
(212) 757-8651
www.evesgarden.com

FANTASY UNLIMITED
102 Pike St.
Seattle, WA 98101
(206) 682-0167

FETISHES BOUTIQUE
704 S.5th St.
Philadelphia, PA 19147
(215) 829-4986
(877) 2CORSET
www.fetishesboutique.com

FORBIDDEN FRUIT
TOY STORE & EDUCATION CENTER
512 Neches St.
Austin, TX 78701
(512) 478-8358

FORBIDDEN FRUIT
FETISH BOUTIQUE
108 N. Loop Blvd.
Austin, TX 78751
(512) 453-8090

FORBIDDEN FRUIT
BODY ART SALON
513 E. Sixth St.
Austin, TX 78751
(512) 476-4596
www.forbiddenfruit.com

GOOD FOR HER
175 Harbord St.
Toronto, ON
Canada, M5S 1H3
(416) 588-0900
(877) 588-0900
www.goodforher.com

GOOD VIBRATIONS
1210 Valencia St.
San Francisco, CA 94110
(415) 974-8980
1620 Polk St.
San Francisco, CA 94109
(415) 974-8985
2504 San Pablo Ave.
Berkley, CA 94702
(510) 841-8987
Mail Order (800) 289- 8423
www.goodvibes.com

INTIMACIES
28 Center St.
Northampton, MA 01060
(413) 582-0709
www.intimaciesonline.com

IT'S MY PLEASURE
4258 SE Hawthorne Blvd.
Portland, OR 97215
(503) 236-0505

LOVECRAFT
27 Yorkville Ave.
Toronto, ON
Canada, M5R 1B7
(416) 923-7331
(877) 923-7331
2200 Dundas St., E.
Mississauga, ON
Canada, L4X 2V3
(905) 276-5772
www.lovecraftsexshop.com

PASSION FLOWER
4 Yosemite Ave.
Oakland, CA 94611
(510) 601-7750

PLEASURE CHEST
7733 Santa Monica Blvd.
West Hollywood, CA 90046
(800) 75 DILDO
(323) 650-1022
www.thepleasurechest.com

PLEASURE PALACE
277 Dalhousie St.
Ottawa, ON
Canada, K1N 7E5
(613) 789-7866

PLEASURE PLACE
1710 Connecticut Ave. NW
Washington, D.C. 20009
www.pleasureplace.com

PURPLE PASSION
242 W. 16th St.
New York, NY 10011
(212) 807-0486
www.purplepassion.com

RUBBER TREE
4426 Burke Avenue N.
Seattle, WA 98103
(206) 663-4750

SH!
22 Coronet St.
London N1 UK
(0171) 613-5456

SIN
4426 Burke Ave. N.
Seattle, WA 98103
(206) 663-4750

SPARTACUS LEATHERS
300 S.W. 12th St.
Portland, OR 97205
(503) 224-2604

THE STOCKROOM
4649 ½ Russell Ave.
Los Angeles, CA 90027
(213) 666-2121
(800) 755-TOYS
www.stockroom.com

STORMY LEATHER
1158 Howard St.
San Francisco, CA 94103
(415) 626-1672
(877) 975-5577
www.stormyleather.com

TOYS IN BABELAND
711 E. Pike St.
Seattle, WA 98122
(206) 328-2914
94 Rivington St.
New York, NY 10002
(212) 375-1701
Mail Order (800) 685-9119
www.babeland.com

VENUS ENVY
1598 Barrington St.
Halifax, Nova Scotia
Canada, B3J 1Z6
(902) 422-0004
www.venusenvy.ns.ca

A WOMAN'S TOUCH
600 Williamson St.
Madison, WI 53703
(888) 621-8880
(608) 250-1928
www.a-womans-touch.com

WOMYN'S WARE
896 Commercial Dr.
Vancouver, BC
Canada, U5L 3Y5
(888) WYM-WARE
(604) 254-2543
www.womynsware.com